TRUE NATURE

CONNECTING WITH NATURE, SPIRIT AND HEART TO MOVE BEYOND THE ILLUSION OF SEPARATION

Thomas Schorr-kon

Copyright © 2018 Thomas Schorr-kon

All rights reserved.

ISBN: **9781790581160**

DEDICATION

For those who are no longer with us who continue to inspire and teach us. For those who are yet to come that we might leave them a more loving society and a greater reverence for nature. For those of us here now, that we may fully live. To followers of nature everywhere.

CONTENTS

	Acknowledgments	vi
1	Coming Home	8
2	Conversations With Nature	51
3	Stalking Oneness	83
4	Science and Shamanism	107
5	Warrior of the heart	127
6	Infrequently asked questions	188
7	Sacred and Wild	205

ACKNOWLEDGMENTS

With thanks to my many teachers: Firstly my family, my mother Ruscha and father Stephan and brothers and sisters Ben, Charlie, Rosy, Sofia. Also to my grandparents especially Lotty and Matuta . To my children Amber, Helix and Otis and their mothers: Jewels Wingfield and Virginia Farman. To my uncles and aunts: Ursula Mommens, Norman Mommens, Patience Grey and Peter Miller. To Dan and Lulu Russel and their children.
To Tom Brown Jr, Nathan Menaged, Philip Carr Gom, John Young, Sal Glencarelle, Andy Nation, Leo Rutherford, Randolph Wolf wind.
To fellow walkers of the path: Adam Barker , Peter Owen Jones and Mac Macartney.
To all the students I have reminded of the beauty of nature and the vastness of spirit. To those I hold as friends: Silas Mosbacher, Simon Carey Morgan, Ariel Blue, Geoff Mcmillan B.E.M., Philip Greenwood, Dave Goodman, Feathers, Anna Richardson, Victoria Mew, Rob Fallon, Caspar Brown, Yan Thompson, Xray John and the rest too numerous to mention here. To Nature and Spirit.

CHAPTER 1

COMING HOME

"Nature is not a place to visit, it is home"

Gary Snyder the practice of the wild

I had been running and was up on the hills surrounding Bristol; I looked down on the M32, tiny cars were hurrying to and fro. From here I could always get some perspective. I had found a book that had been recommended to me a year before and I was about to run an experiment from one of the manuals written by the same author. I was going to try out something called fox walking and splatter vision. The book The Tracker by Tom Brown JR had given me a focused starting point that anchored the esoteric and the practical. Having read many books on Shamanism that mentioned in passing tracking and stalking more as spiritual practice than as a grounded physical activity.

I began my experiment taking eight to ten steps and to my great surprise met a fox head on. I had been running that route for several years and had never seen a fox there before. I was awe struck what I had been reading about was coming to life.

I have had a few experiences where a book I was reading has come of the page, but this encounter was indelible. This opened the door to many life changing experiences of connecting with nature energy and spirit in ways that were beyond what I had thought possible.

It was not long after this that my father went on a trip to Australia where he drowned. It was an immense shock and wake up call. He drowned saving the life of a German woman who got into trouble in the rip currents on a beach where they were swimming with no life guard; a beach he had swum with dolphins on the previous year.

Having miraculously escaped from Poland during the Second World War from Nazi Germany thanks to the extreme courage of his mother it seemed poignant even ironic that he died saving a German woman.

He had always told us to follow our hearts and in the aftermath of grief and shock at his passing the only thing that offered a thread of interest out of the maze of grief were the books I had been reading by Tom Brown Jr, so I decided to go and study with him in America.

This began an Odyssey of awakening not only in my connection with nature but also in my personal and spiritual growth. Some aspects of which occurred before I got to Tom Brown Jr's school, leaving me with powerful experiences that I could not explain away. The most lasting spiritual experiences I have had have been the ones that reflected me back to myself that allow a clear view of the self.

After my initial training I felt for the first time that I truly lived on the planet, that where ever I trod was my home. I realised that I had wanted this feeling since as a child I had run wild and free in the forests of my youth.

The Earth spoke to me through the tracks left by her creatures, there were plants for food and every possible ailment, I could make fire by rubbing sticks together and build a shelter from sticks and leaves to keep me warm down to minus twenty. I could move as silently as a fox and slip into the flow of nature. I could find plants to make string and rope, make cloth from hide and tools from stone and bone.

I was no longer an alien, disconnected and alone but surrounded by living beings, be they plant or animal. It was a revelation, a healing of the modern condition of disconnection and disinterest; I was filled with energy and a hunger to know more.

BUSHCRAFT SHAMAN

Something was driving my need to know what went on beyond the veil of the physical; I craved to know what the shamans really knew. The fascination with all things magical had been there from an early age. I had had a dream in which a terrifying dragon had appeared and the only way out of the dream was to leap into its jaws. This left me with a fascination for dragons.

My interest in Spirit was further stoked by reading accounts of Native American medicine stories that somehow seemed to come at the magical through the natural rather than the occult (which always brought up fear and felt like a closed symbol to me.) I later encountered the approach of the Druids which seemed more in alignment with what I had learned of the medicine teachings.

I took up meditation as a teenager following simple Tibetan Buddhist guidelines and when I found very similar aspects talked about by Native American medicine people and Tibetan Buddhist's it confirmed at least theoretically that piercing the veil may be possible.

Yet the main driving factor was an experience that occurred while I was in college it left me with the need to discover how to help my fellow sisters and brothers when they are struggling at the edge of spiritual discovery or mental breakdown, as it tends to be categorised in our society

THE INITIATION

Death had played an important role in moving me along my path several times before these events. It was becoming clear to me that death acted like a gateway an initiation both for the dead and the living.

The first death and possibly the one that affected me the most was in my final year of college. I had made a number of friends outside the art school where I was training to paint and sculpt who I spent most of my time with. One was a young aspiring black poet Eugine, with whom I shared an active interest in meditation. Another was Yewan who shared my passion for martial arts and also had an interest in the esoteric.

It was the final summer holiday before the last year and two good friends of mine invited me to travel to Greece with them. My friend

TRUE NATURE

Yewan had recently been sectioned into a mental hospital diagnosed with Drug induced psychosis. Admittedly he was becoming a little unstable. Experiencing bursts of ecstatic synchronistic experiences. It was like he was storming heaven. In these states he seemed connected to knowing things he could not otherwise have access to. Yet he was not in control of his state, it served to unbalance him. His time in the mental institution was a death knell for him. They fed him with far more powerful drugs than he had been taking previously. His state seemed to be reduced from this almost angelic expanded experience to the densest state of consciousness, the lowest common denominator. He seemed wooden his skin bursting with acne from the toxicity of the drugs he was taking. Throughout this period I stood by and watched this terrifying transformation taking place. While trying to do what I could to help. This was pitifully little. I felt helpless not knowing how to help, feeling totally out of my depth.

Later his parents came to take him home telling him that they had never understood him. It was only later, after his return home that I heard he had committed suicide.

These events created a powerful after shock in my life and amongst the mutual friends we shared. I resonated very deeply with my friend, and was aware of the inadequacies in my ability to genuinely help. I felt that he had strayed into a realm that gave him access to powerful insight yet in an unbalanced way.

The seismic effect of this sent me into a deep process of first the destruction of my self-concept and the then subsequent "remembering" i.e. putting back together of myself with a new paradigm at the core. The main demon this unleashed was that of fear. To be overwhelmed with fear to feel it in everything that you do is petrifying, in that it holds you motionless like ice, unable to act.

One of the things that I vividly remember from that time is the fear I felt when someone knocked on my front door. I recently discovered how the experience of feeling afraid when someone knocks on the door, related to my recent ancestral past. As during the Second World

War both my parents, in very different circumstances, faced a very real threat from such a situation.

Many things contributed to the thawing process, the gesture of a shaman, the love and healing of parents, even the sacred relations with a power plant. Yet this death began a journey for me of transformation and empowerment, shaking the very foundations of my world-view to make room for one that is far larger and more alive.

To me this death was a gateway and an abyss that took me through the darkness to the light.

One of the pledges that I made during this time was that I would learn enough about how my friend had stormed his way into heaven to be able to help any friend of mine who strayed there in the future.

When I returned to England after taking my first steps at being able to enter and work directly with spirit. Having discovered where my friend had strayed and possible ways to enter and move safely around in these other states. The first situation I encountered was a friend of my brothers who whilst in India had been given a powerful experience with a guru that he had as yet been unable to integrate. In terms of the established view of things he was considered to be going crazy. There was a powerful echo of my friend's suicide, parents though loving, not really understanding what was going on for their son. Possibly the fear this generated, creating more confusion as to what they could do. Things were reaching a critical point for this friend. He similarly had access to realms of insight and sensitivity beyond the flesh, yet in a turbulent and ungrounded way. I had been shown a way to ground and protect others and set about performing a ceremony with this as the focus. It was as if the terms of my pledge were being tested. I ran a ceremony with my mother also present in the garden of her house. During the ceremony a fox came within arm's reach of our circle oblivious to our presence. This friend, as I write over 20 years on is still with us and doing very well. He is now married and settled.

NEED TO KNOW

After the revelation of feeling like I was coming home to the Earth I suddenly wanted to know all there was to know about living on this beautiful planet. My childlike curiosity was given such a jolt that I began to question everything. I had so many questions and became hungry to know about everything.

Natural history became my passion, plants, animals, weather patterns, stars and crafts that made it possible to live for longer periods out in the wilds. I experienced a kind of overwhelm as there seemed so much that I did not know. It took a while for me to realise that there was a lifetime of mysteries to be unraveled and that each discovery could be savoured rather than rushing to know everything. I still relish the questions that I don't know the answers to that provoke further homework or finding the answer out with a student or friend.

My interest in Spirit was also driving me. Understanding how this was an aspect of our natural state and that we have just not been shown how to access this, allowed me to practice these skills without fear. Being shown how spirit is also alive in Nature and how to develop a deep relationship with it shaped the paradigm I began to follow. I began to experience how we are entwined with our environment on many levels.

I was recently talking to a Hawaiian friend who told me he was related to the indigenous people of his island. He proceeded to tell me how his ancestors worshiped the rocks, waters, winds and sun. I stopped him and asked him, Do you worship your brothers and sisters and your parents?" he thought this was rather an odd question. I then went on to say that worshiping something can make it seem like it is really far away. As if it were a deity up in the heavens or deep in the ocean somehow beyond reach. I suggested that perhaps his ancestors felt more as if these aspects were their relations and so they did not necessarily deify them but offered them thanksgiving, respect and awe, and were in a more direct day to day relationship with them. He seemed to like this as it brought him closer both to his ancestors and to his own grounded connection with the earth.

FEAR OF THE DARK

It has always seemed strange to me how we cast certain aspects of nature in a negative light. We have the big bad wolf and the deep dark woods that always have connotations of lurking evil and disaster. Even the nature of the dark is perceived as evil. Yet I have witnessed many times how children once they realise that the shadows are the best place to hide lose their fear of the dark in one evening in the woods. Instead of being fearful of the dark they end up spending hours stalking from one dark patch to another to get as close to those watching from the light of the fire as they can. It is in essence the fear of the unknown that elicits a visceral response to want to destroy the object of our fear. When this is turned towards nature then we find we are demonising the very thing that nourish and support us. As what we fear we seek to destroy. Conversely what we love we seek to protect. This understanding has always underpinned my teaching, so that I have encouraged people to fall in love with the Earth so they will protect her. It is very similar with our inner journey, many aspects are catagorised as demonic and negative and yet what determines how we are affected by these forces is the quality of our relationship to the so called negative.

"Evil must never be fought with rage or hatred, for that will only make it stronger. You must never fear the evil ones, for your fear will consume and destroy you. Instead, fight the evil spirits with love and compassion, for those are our greatest weapons." Tom Brown Jr

I have been constantly surprised by experiences that have unfolded on my inner journey. The experiences that happened before I started training I wrote of as bizarre unexplainable coincidence. Only after I started to understand the language of spirit did these I see these occurrences as powerful building blocks of understanding and faith. Listening to the messages of spirit and acting on them yielded meaningful and moving results.

DEATH MIDWIFERY

I sat on the fourteenth floor of an upper Manhattan block in my Cousin Peter's apartment. I was between classes I had just finished what still to this day was one of the hardest barriers for me to penetrate. To look into my own shadow to see what would take me off the path of light. The experience left me reeling. I felt I could not go on with the work. I was blocked. The images that had presented themselves had been to painful and dark. My fear of physical violence and the return from a state of abject terror that had occurred in response to the suicide of my friend Yewan felt like nothing in the face of this supernatural fear. I was in a state of spiritual shock. I was trying to decide whether to quit my training go home and try to forget that I had ever begun this journey.

As I sat I felt a presence come into the room. I felt it to be my grandmother. She quietly explained that I need to go and see her friend Miriam and tell her that she would be there to help her friend to the other side, she would help her cross over to the other side..

I was in a state of wonderment this was the first contact I had had with a dead ancestor. What was most surprising to me was that it was unsought, it was unexpected. It was not a major apparition, it was a sense that I had of my grandmother, but the message was clear as a bell. With this now ringing in my head, pushing aside the other thoughts of ending my training I set about seeing if I could visit Miriam.

After the experience the doubts began to slip in. Was I just making it up? Or had it really happened. After some deliberation I resolved to follow through, to at least try and deliver the message.

I contacted Miriam's daughter who was herself retired and looking after Miriam. I discovered that Miriam had been bed ridden for a year. I had been coming to train for the past two years in New Jersey passing through New York each time and had not even thought to get in contact with her. So I organised a visit for tea.

When I arrived I met with Miriam's daughter and her husband and had a very pleasant tea catching up and passing on stories of the family. As the afternoon progressed I began to grow increasingly anxious, dreading the task I had come to perform. Not knowing if I would have the courage to pass on the message. The time came and I was brought to see Miriam. As I went towards her bed I was engulfed in an atmosphere of fear bordering on terror. The phrase that still rings in my head is "I am a f***ing New Yorker I am not going to die".

As we talked her attitude softened and we began to reminisce, yet she repeated herself and told me about people that I had not known. She told me how she would like to take one last trip out to have tea somewhere in town and I told her I would take her the next time I was in the city. After we had been talking for some time, all along the tension was building in me that the time had come to share the message I had come to deliver. I took my courage in both hands and said,

"You know my Grandmother, your good friend will be there to take you to the other side when you die". It felt as if the inevitability of death could just not be mentioned especially in this powerful atmosphere of denial. My message was met with blankness on the surface, yet I could feel it going in deeply perhaps even reaching the target of her heart. Perhaps it would give Miriam the courage to let go. We continued our conversation as if nothing had passed between us, yet I felt the seed of my statement would unfold in those quiet moments of reflection. I felt relief that I had managed to convey my grandmother's message to her friend, relief that when spirit had asked me to fulfil a task I had undertaken it. All was now left to trust, to surrender.

After this I could continue to focus on the question of my continuing training. I eventually came to the conclusion that I would go back taking each day at a time. If I felt to leave I would. With this approach I managed to complete the course that I had intended to, broadening my understanding of the relationship with the dark teachers and the need for integrating their lessons.

Two weeks after my return my mother phoned me, she had received a letter from Miriam's daughter saying that she had passed away shortly after my visit.

This experience of death midwifery was the first experience of its kind for me and has formed a powerful building block in my belief in spirit. There have been many other experiences of this type over the years and each one has helped me to form a very different relationship to death.

BLIND MEN

When I arrived back from New York after the intense training and the experience with my Grandmother's spirit, I was looking forward to the comforts of home.

I was at the time living with two friends and had left them in charge of the house. As I came in through the front door the sense of peaceful welcome that I had been looking forward to was shattered. I could feel the atmosphere charged with animosity. It was as if an energetic battle had been raging throughout the communal space. No one was home yet the psychic aftermath was almost visible.

After settling in and resting I needed to know what had been going on and what to do about it. Not really knowing where to start I decided to head out to the woods to seek the council of the trees.

As I headed into the woods I began to think about my two friends, both of whom were interested in self-development. They were both training in different practices, following their unique journeys through life with a commitment to growth. In this I felt we were all similar. We were all developing relationship with life on as many levels as we could. All of us held a strong belief in the sacred nature of it all. Yet here we were the two of them not talking to each other, and having created a great deal of disruption to the fabric of energy in the house.

I moved into an area of the woods where I had watched a family of heron's nesting high up in a mature oak tree some months before. I found myself drawn to an area and sat for a while.

I began to use one of the new ways I had recently learned, tree preaching. As I spoke out to the natural world around me I felt the weight of concerns lifting from me. After checking on the heron's I returned to the car park. As I emerged from the undergrowth a story came to me. I could not remember where I had come across it before, but the echo of it in my mind could not be silenced. It was the story of the three blind men and the elephant.

The story tells of three blind men who have never seen an elephant. Their friend thinks that as a treat it would be fun for them to experience an elephant. So in turn they are lead to different parts of the elephant's body. One is led to the trunk one to the ear and one to the tail. They all get together afterwards and a huge argument ensues, they almost get into a fight. The first one who has felt the trunk describes the elephant as similar to a powerful snake. The second who felt the ear says that the elephant is like a big cool leafy grove. While the third tells of a piece of rope tied to a tree trunk. Each one claims that his experience of the elephant is true and therefore that the others are not.

I found myself laughing out loud at the absurdity and clarity that the story provoked in relation to my situation. Let's face it, this is the story of many religions and their relationships with each other. Though I am certain they would disagree.

Later I managed to share the story with one of my cohabitants and he too found it to be as funny and hopefully as insightful.

COMING HOME

"Look deep into nature, and then you will understand everything better." Albert Einstein

By introducing some of the fundamental survival skills I hope to show that Earth skills are intricate activities that can enrich our lives and bring great peace and satisfaction. If we are feeling disconnected in this technological age then developing these physical skills reconnects us directly to the elements. The awareness skills bring us into the present open our senses and bringing them back to life, bringing us back to life.

In unravelling the language of nature we notice the gifts the plants and animals give us. We connect to the universality of living on the earth, with the wider non-human communities. We also connect with many and ancient cultures through the ways of earth living and survival as we find they exist as the foundation of all cultures. Through this we are brought in touch with all humanity. Appreciating how our ancestors lived, we can understand where many of our innate needs and desires spring from, finding ways to integrate and appropriately utilise these instinctive drives.

Our ancestors have thrived on earth for so long by careful use of the available resources and patient observation of nature, when we tap into this legacy we feel that we have come home to the Earth.

The relationship that forms with nature develops our appreciation and gratitude. We can see ourselves with our cultural baggage stripped away. Able to let go of what no longer serves us as we are caught up in the joy of discovering the hidden worlds around us. Inspired to play with our natural energy and develop our sensitivity.

We begin to study our own back yard noticing the many signs of life that we may have missed. After a while we realise that in studying our own back yard we are gaining a transferable understanding that can be applied to any other environment on earth. With this our sense of being lost evaporates. We start to feel at home on the earth. With our feet firmly planted on the earth we can explore the energies within and around us in nature then the doorway to spirit swings open.

SHELTERING FROM THE SKY

MAKING OUR HOME IN THE WORLD

It was a routine shelter building exercise, I had explained how the Native peoples had observed the squirrels, who hibernate through the winter, constructing their shelters of sticks and leaves. Squirrels make tight balls of leaves that they wedge into the branches of a tree. The keen observers of nature had then devised a simple skeletal structure of sticks that when covered in two feet of leaves and debris forms a water tight warm shelter. So we set of to find a good location to build one.

We were looking for an abundance of materials. No dangerous overhanging branches, somewhere free from insects and ticks, and an area that was not prone to flash flooding or excessive dampness. The group began construction and within the hour had completed their shelter. As we finished it one member of the group was overwhelmed with emotion and began to cry.

'I feel at home on the earth for the first time' she shared with us. 'Where ever I go I can make a home' she said.

This experience was a gift for the whole group and it reminded me of the first time I to had had this feeling. The longing to feel closer to nature had been in me since I was a child and for me it had come on the completion of the first course that I took with one of my most influential mentors, Tom Brown JR. I emerged from the sweat lodge the week's intensive teaching filling my thoughts and spilling over through my heart with gratitude to Tom and his teacher Stalking Wolf. I lay prone on the Earth arms out stretched as if hugging her. I was home, I felt like I belonged to the Earth, no longer an alien, able to go anywhere and feel at home.

If we consider the principle involved in any skill we can adapt it to suit whatever our circumstances are. So we need to discover what we actually need from our shelter. We are seeking to prevent the greatest killer of the outdoors which is exposure. This we can die of within hours, thus making the finding of a sheltered spot or the creation of a full scale survival shelter the number one survival priority. We can still attend to any other priority if opportunity presents, I.e. we come across some edible plants or a water source while we search for an appropriate site. We want to be both sheltered from exposure to the elements and to be able to maintain an appropriate temperature. When we discover that making fire from natural materials is a sophisticated skill we perhaps start to wonder how we can keep ourselves warm without having to make fire. The answer to this is simply about finding materials that trap air to increase their insulation value. This combined with the ability of materials to shed water becomes our focus in the creation of viable shelters. As our skill with fire making increases we may consider shelters that incorporate a fire. Which tend to be more open and use the reflected heat of the fire to maintain warmth rather than just the insulating qualities of the materials.

The final consideration is the conservation of energy. As we observe nature we discover that conserving energy is at the core of much animal behaviour that to us may seem like laziness. The lion resting for long periods after a feed, a lizard warming itself on a rock etc… One way that this is expressed in shelter building is in the selection of the site. We are seeking the most favourable conditions for our shelter. If we can find a situation where we need to do little work or natural elements provide aspects that we would otherwise have to manufacture we can try to incorporate them into our shelter. This reduces the amount of energy we expend and therefore puts us in a better position. The description that follows offers guidelines that can be adapted depending on the terrain and natural features.

Choice of site:

1. Near available materials.
2. Choose a high and flat well drained area.
3. A transitional area is best, using the edge of a wood rather than deep in the overgrowth, to benefit from sunlight and species diversity.
4. Awareness of compass directions, Considering prevailing winds, and overall exposure to sunlight. Door facing east for best results in Europe putting the south westerly prevailing wind at the back of the shelter. Avoid North face of hills as little sunlight falls making everything much damper.
5. Be aware of potential water flow if there is a serious down pour, for

example avoid dry river beds and wet areas.
6. 50 meters from a water source, far enough away to be clear of dampness, possible flooding and risk of contaminating the water source.
7. Away from: Insects and poisonous or irritating plants.
8. Away from deer bedding areas due to the presence of tics that can carry Lyme's disease.
9. Away from over hanging dead branches (widow makers)Beech especially.
10. Make use of natural shelters and existing features especially where appropriate.

CLOTHING PRIMARY SHELTER

Our first available shelter is our clothing, so we might make choices of what we wear based on the survival value of the fabric. Cotton for example does not retain any thermal value when it gets wet, while wool and silk on the other hand do. Merino wool is fine enough to wear against the skin and it wicks away moisture so does not pick up the smell of sweat readily and helps to regulate temperature, keeping you cool in the heat and warm when it is cold. Because it wicks moisture away it does not need washing as often as cotton.

We might also look at the surface having some camouflage value. Not necessarily wearing a camouflage pattern but moving away from single colour fabrics and choosing patterns that help to blend in.

As far as survival fabrics go the best is buckskin. This is deer hide with the hair and membranes removed and dressed with brains. Though a simple grass blankets made from bundles of grass tied together can be turned into a cloak easily. Grass is a hollow fiber hence a great insulator. The Ice man Otzi who lived over five thousand years ago was discovered in the Alps in 1991 was wearing a grass cloak.

SHELTER CONSTRUCTION

There are many types of shelter the most useful to learn first is a shelter that can keep you both warm and dry without the need for a fire. The debris hut is really a waterproof sleeping bag made of sticks and leaves. Just burrowing into a big pile of leaves or cut grasses would keep us warm even if they were a bit damp. But we want to avoid getting wet if possible.

1. Clear site to bear ground to avoid lying on roots and to check for the presence of insects nests.

2. Select a strong main beam. At least as tall as you with your arm held above your head plus an additional foot in length or (30 centimeters). The beam should be at least as thick as your upper arm.

3. Either create supports or find something to support the main beam on. This should be supported at crotch height to give enough room to enter and create minimal air gaps. The simplest support structure is a tripod. To create this find 2 strong forked sticks that can support the main beam.

4. If necessary lash tripod in place. Lay down under the tripod to make certain you will fit. Continue doing this throughout the process. Decide where the door is going to be.

5. Then begin laying on "ribs" over the frame. These can be dead wood. Cover at least one side then fill the inside with preferably dry leaf litter, grass, ferns etc.. to create a dry and warm bed inside. The debris does not necessarily need to be dry to keep you warm but is more comfortable that way.

6. Finish laying ribs on. Build igloo door to reduce warm air loss.

7. Cover with two feet of leaf litter or foliage all over.

https://www.udemy.com/bushcraft-survival-1/ This link gives access to a video course that has a free video showing the construction of a shelter at speed. All the other basic skills are covered in detail on this course.

Most types of shelter are constructed in a similar fashion though many other materials can be used.

THE LESSONS

Shelter building as a group brings to the fore the interaction between the group members, it exposes leadership qualities, the capacity to cooperate and share tasks. It makes available to the skillful on looker a good view of the group dynamics. This provides the facilitator with a choice of either allowing what comes up to work itself out or the possibility of skillful intervention in supporting discussion about areas of conflict as personal issues are brought to the surface.

While it can be used as a tool to help to see ourselves more clearly ultimately it is possible to address issues of attitude in a safe environment. As our attitude in a survival situation can either kill us or help us thrive. We need to understand that what we are used to in our everyday lives in terms of our usual annoyances and petty issues expend a great deal of emotional energy, in a survival situation conservation of energy is paramount, so self-mastery in respect of how we manage our feelings is a vital lesson to at least acknowledge. I am not trying to suggest that we shut down, but we see our emotional responses in a broader context, and develop the skills to move into response rather than reaction.

One year course group I was running developed in a very interesting way. There were almost an equal number of men and women and one of the group members wanted to have time in separate gender groups, so we devoted a few hours to this when we met. During our quest preparation weekend the women decided that they wanted to do their survival quest as a group of women separate from the men. I thought this was a very interesting way for the group to go and supported their decision. So it fell to me to broach the subject to the men. It came as a great shock to the men; it was as if the milk of woman kindness had suddenly been withdrawn from them.

The discussion that ensued was most interesting. The women voiced their desire to approach the task without the normally help full skills development and strength that the men exhibited i.e. to rely on their own skills base. The most surprising thing they shared was that with the men around they felt a sense of safety which they would miss, but none the less wanted to face the experience with out that in play, to empower their sense of self-reliance. The men shared that what they would miss was the capacity of the women to communicate with in the groups to bridge the build-up of difficult emotional issues; especially between the various male egos. During the quest the two groups were able to visit each other.

This particular turn of events facilitated a lot of insight within the group as to the dynamics that the participants needed to be aware of in them-selves. This proved to be beneficial to all concerned, bringing to the surface unconscious fears and concerns that transformed into understanding of the qualities of the opposite gender. It was that year that during the quest in the French Pyrenees the first day was tee shirt wearing weather and the next day a foot of snow fell, thoroughly testing the resolve and skill of all concerned.

WATER

MOTHER OF LIFE

Perhaps it was the fasting or the purity of the Scottish country that made the dream so clear. I heard squeals of joy coming from higher up the valley. I met Lulu coming down the path 'everyone is sliding down the waterfall' she said you must come. I started up the path coming into view of the deep pool bellow the waterfall. I saw Dan and my brother Ben sliding down the waterfall, it looked so good I had to try.

I woke with the mist still folded on the ground. My fire was nearly out, yet the beauty of the valley held me in awe. I made my way down to the water's edge and tentatively dipped myself in the water. The cold stole my warmth and any vestige of sleep, the lack of food was affecting my resistance to the cold. The dream was lost in the mist of the morning and I was in and out of the pool with icy speed.

I returned to my spot stoked up the fire and continued to sit. By midday I heard the rustling approach of Dan coming to check up on me. Though we were not supposed to speak he shared with me that for some time he had been thinking about sliding down the waterfall above which I sat. The dream resurfaced clear as day. Dan went to slide down splashing down with such exuberance and aliveness that he immediately went round and did it again. I followed suit twice and the rush and exhilaration of the experience kept me warm and strengthened for the rest of the day. Plunging at speed into the water I had overcome the cold I felt much more present in the location as if the bathing had made me more at one with my environment.

Water is the next survival priority. If we do without water for more than 24 hours we can put ourselves in danger of dehydration. This can cause serious problems for us

Dehydration symptoms:

Increased thirst

Dry mouth and swollen tongue

Weakness

Dizziness

Confusion

Fainting

Decreased urine out put

Inability to sweat

Palpitations

Hallucinations

This obviously puts us at risk especially in a survival situation. It is important to be careful with the purification of water. There are several water borne diseases we have to avoid: Weil's disease caused by animal's urine, cryptosporidium which is a parasite, E coli which is a bacteria from fecal contamination, Giardia another parasite. All of the listed contaminants are killed by boiling. There are other possible contaminants. We also have to consider chemical contamination which is intensified by boiling. We can also get a good idea of the purity of a water source from the plant and animal life in and around the water. Frogs and newts are very sensitive to water contaminants.

<u>Water purification methods:</u>

1. Filtering
2. Distilling Solar still
3. Dew collecting
4. Boiling
5. Catching Rain water
6. Harvesting from plants (Tree tapping and vines)
7. Finding a spring
8. Digging (Indian Well)
9. Aspiration: Trees expelling water through leaves at night.

BIRCH TREE TAPPING 1

BIRCH TREE TAPPING 2

BIRCH TREE TAPPING 3

SOLAR STILL

DRINKING FROM A VINE

FILTERING ROCK BOILED WATER

WATER FILTER

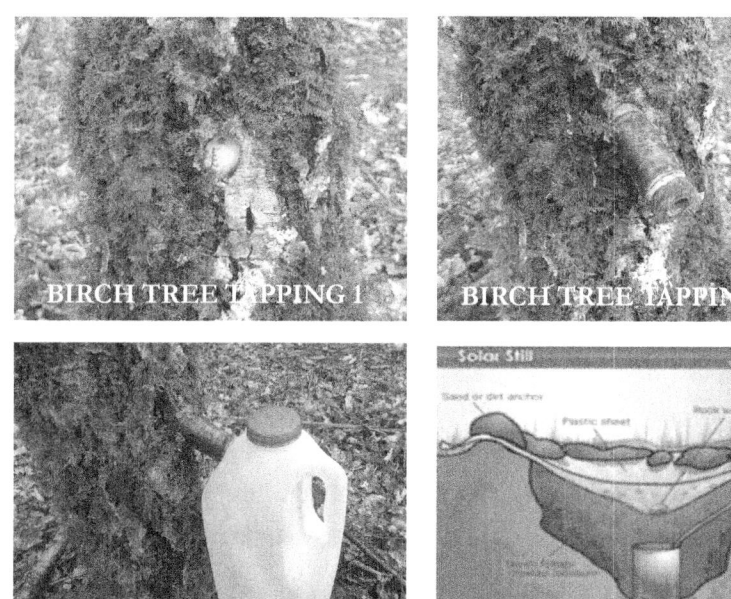

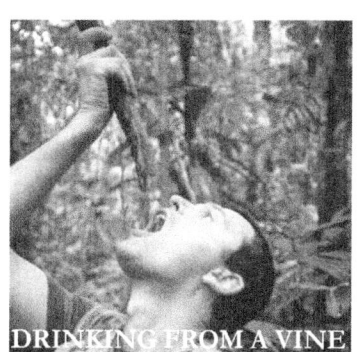

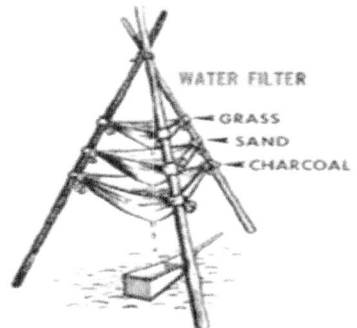

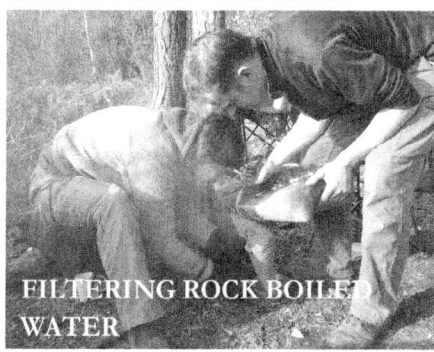

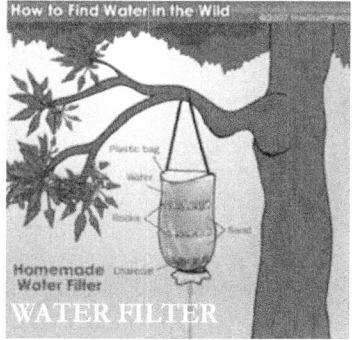

Fifteen years ago I took a group of students to the Amazon I met up with my brother in Iquitos. From there we drove forty kilometers or so down the one road through the jungle. Ben my brother then led us ten kilometers into the jungle with a group of natives including their elder Don Hilber the eighty year old son of one of Peru's most famous shaman. We were headed to the Yacumamy reserve started by the head of anthropology at Cambridge University at the time, Francois Freedman.

We camped in the jungle for a week using up our supplies quickly and having to rely on hunting and foraging from the forest. The locals knew a great deal about the forest and were surprised and delighted to show us what they knew. At one point a neighbouring hunter turned up wearing a back pack he had made from weaving two palm fronds together. Excitedly a few of us asked him to show us how he did it. He was so delighted that he re-tied his back pack in several different ways to show us how to do it.

A small river ran by the side of the camp which the locals swam in and drank directly from. It was also a great source of fishing, mostly piranhas as it turned out. At one point I sat with my rod that was a simple branch patiently waiting. A large fly landed on my knee which I swiftly swatted. I subsequently put it on the hook and whipped out a piranha. Better to be eating them than the other way round I thought.

I figured that if the locals could drink the water directly then so could I. I also tried drinking and swimming at the same time as if I could not do that in such a pure wilderness as the Amazon rain forest there would not be any where I could do it.

What was most interesting was that several of the students who came with me were almost obsessive about using their reverse osmosis filters to purify the water. One of the guys got terribly sick with Guardia and found the walk out of the jungle to be the most difficult thing he had to accomplish up to that time.

By the hut we stayed in there was a lime tree, and periodically I would add the juice to my water just to add some flavour.

When I returned home I started to have some unpleasant symptoms. While I was on the phone to my friend Francois Freedman she said 'did I remember to tell you to eat lime pips if you got Guardia?' I replied that she had not mentioned it. As soon as I put the phone down I went to the kitchen to see if I had any limes. All I could find were lemons. I duly ate two lemon pips by the next day my symptoms had gone. I have since discovered how grapefruit and its seed extract are used to treat many intestinal parasites and even used against cholera.

For many years after this I used Grapefruit seed extract as a prophylactic for myself and my family against water borne disease. Then while spending time in India I ate some street food during the monsoon and came down with a forty eight hour bug during which time I lost 3 kilos, it was not an experience I wished to repeat, and lemon pips and grapefruit seed extract had no effect. It was not until the next year when I was back in India and started using a single drop of Oregano oil in a small amount of milk that has helped get rid of even the most severe bugs. I have also found Thyme essential oil will do the same.

VIKTOR SHAUBERG WATER WIZARD

We are more than 70% water so its importance to our normal functioning is paramount. Whether we are in hot or cold climates we need it for our bodies to function properly.

"When drunk as melted snow-water, it also gives rise to certain deficiencies and if no other water is available on occasion can result in goitre, the enlargement of the thyroid gland"

living energies Callum Coates p 114

Good water is the basis of good health both for us and all other species. There are many anomalies and interesting scientific aspects of water that make life possible.

Water molecules do not have straight atomic connections but the hydrogen and oxygen atoms are held together by curved connections. Water is also considered as the universal solvent as most things dissolve in it.

Our blood is 90% water and it is interesting to discover how our body temperature is largely determined by the water in our system.

"Water is most temperature stable at +37.5 centigrade making it most resistant to external temperature fluctuations of heat or cold at our normal blood temperature."

living energies Callum Coates p 113

This is one of the reasons we need to keep hydrated in cold environments so our body temperature remains stable.

Viktor Shauberg instead of going to university went into the forest for a year to study nature and discovered many interesting aspects of how water flows and how when it adsorbs carbon and minerals it then forces its way up to the surface flowing out as springs, hence carbonated water.

"Were we to drink pure H2O constantly, it would quickly leach out all our store of minerals and trace elements, debilitating and ultimately killing us."

Shauberg also observed that the core of a river was warmer and denser than other areas of the river in his study of flow. He eventually created flow forms that mimic the natural vortices and directions of flow that water will take in an undisturbed stream. He theorised that water gets purified and energised by these movements.

"While all fluids become consistently and steadily denser with cooling, water, alone reaches its densest state at a temperature of +4 degrees Celsius (39.2 Fahrenheit). This is the so called 'anomaly point'.... below this temperature it once more expands......this anomalous expansion below +4 0C is vital to the survival of fish life....as it freezes into ice it is less dense and therefore floats creating an insulating layer for the fish." P 111

THE LESSONS

The lessons of water are profound and as multifaceted as the drops of rain that bless us when it rains.

"When water is still, it is like a mirror, reflecting the beard and the eyebrows. It gives the accuracy of the water-level, and the philosopher makes it his model. And if water thus derives lucidity from stillness, how much more the faculties of the mind? The mind of the Sage being in repose becomes the mirror of the universe, the speculum of all creation."

Alan W. Watts, Tao: The Watercourse Way

BECOMING THE WATER

It was a clear star lit night and I was preparing to enter the cleansing lodge. Similar to a sweat lodge only with just four stones and one enters alone sitting in the place of honour opposite the door. The ceremony was being undertaken under the skilful tutelage of ceremonial leader in the Lakota tradition. I entered the lodge and my partner was tending the fire for me outside as I had done for her previously.

I sat in meditation for nearly half an hour trying really hard to connect to spirit. Nothing had happened and I began to feel abandoned by the 'Tungashilas', the spirits of the directions. It was at this point that I surrendered; I gave up trying and lay down and curled up like a stone. I decided to become stone. It was at this point that I felt the wind start to blow, and it blew me up into the clouds and I suddenly became a cloud, no longer feeling the sense of human presence that I normally feel in my body, but a broader softer sense of being, more amorphous. Just as I was beginning to adjust to this strange sense of cloudness I was fired down as lightening. A most indescribably charged electrifying experience. It was so exhilarating that as I came back to cloud consciousness I asked to be fired down again as lightening. By the third time the cloud had moved me on and we travelled at speed on the wind far across the land scape. Later I began to fall like rain and it felt like somewhere between a bliss full weight less floating with that delightful feeling you get in your belly when you go over a humped back bridge at speed. I have not been able to be upset about it raining since as it reminds me of the freefalling bliss of the rain drops.

I was then drunk by a human and unceremoniously peed into the sewage system until I ended up flowing into the rivers and re-joining the sea. I made my way far out into the ocean and then was recalled back to the cloud.

My partner had been sitting outside the lodge the whole time and had witnessed the actual wind picking up and a huge weather front of cloud sweep across the otherwise clear night sky at the same time as I was blown up into the clouds in my vision.

WILD FIRE

THE SPARK OF LIFE

I recently observed a student learning to make wild fire on one of my classes. As we get out the materials there is usually a scrum for the 'best' bits. I observed a particular student selecting his pieces with care. He moved away from the rest of the group to carefully craft his pieces. Frantic activity took over for several hours. Bows spun, spindles squeaked, smoke rose, char dust collected until a few tinder bundles ignited. Then we moved on to the next subject we needed to cover.

I watched as in ever available spare moment the student would get out his bow drill and make another attempt. Each time with a calm and collected attitude that felt like he was confident he was going to make fire. He was not concerned about making fire first there was almost a savouring of the whole experience. As if engaged in something sacred, something he had wanted to do for a long time but he was not hurrying towards the goal.

As I observed this I realised that this was the right attitude to accomplish the task. I knew he would make fire too. Unlike those who had made it so quickly he would also have the learning of his mistakes and observations. So his future attempts would be made easier. At lunch time on the last day again he got out his bow drill and within a few moments his tinder bundle was in flames. He is no longer a student of mine but an accomplished caretaker of the Earth and a dear friend.

Fire has huge implications in survival from keeping warm, purifying water, cooking, making tools and utensils to signalling for help. It is also like having a companion a friend a living entity a grandfather present with you.

I first read about making wild fire in Brian Bates's book 'The Way of Wyrd' and was inspired from then on to want to make wild fire. Ten years later I was hunched over a bow drill kit of fresh Cedar, making piles of brown dust and smoke learning that there certainly is smoke without fire. For four days I practiced trying again and again in every spare moment. Until that fantastic moment came when the ambition I had held for ten years was realised, taking the glowing ember in the cradle of the tinder bundle and nursing it into flame. Realising that my relationship to fire was forever changed, I could conjure wild fire coaxing it from the wood to the flame, bringing it to life from dead wood.

In order to write this I went back to Brian's book to re-read what had inspired me twenty years before and perhaps to quote some part of the text. I had to read it several times when I found it, because the method described and the choice of wood, all fall far short of getting anywhere close to making fire. When I re-read the section that had so inspired me I felt dejected and cheated. The spark of inspiration that had lit a fire inside me was based on a fantasy, false information. It took a while for me to realise that the spark of inspiration that his description had lit in me had created the desire to accomplish this skill even if the information was incorrect, and that ember still burns in my heart today.

There are many methods of fire making friction fire lighting being the most universal and least terrain dependent.

- Spark: Flint and steel

- Friction: Bow drill, hand drill, mouth drill, fire plough, pump drill, fire thong.

- Compression: Fire piston.

- Electrical spark: battery and wire wool. Car battery.

- Chemical: potassium permanganate, matches.

- Refraction: Lens.

- Focusing light: parabolic reflector.

TRUE NATURE

SELECTION OF FIRE PISTONS

FIRE PISTON IN ACTION

REFRACTION LENS

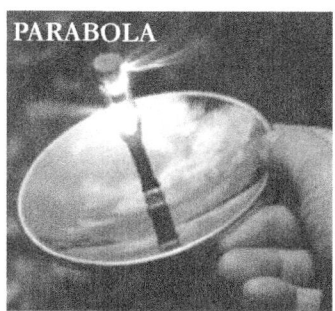

PARABOLA

BURNING IN

MARKING THE NOTCH

CARVING THE NOTCH

MAKING A COAL

REMOVING THE COAL FROM THE NOTCH

BLOWING THE TINDER BUNDLE TO FLAME

PUTTING THE BUNDLE INTO THE TIPI FIRE

FLINT AND STEEL

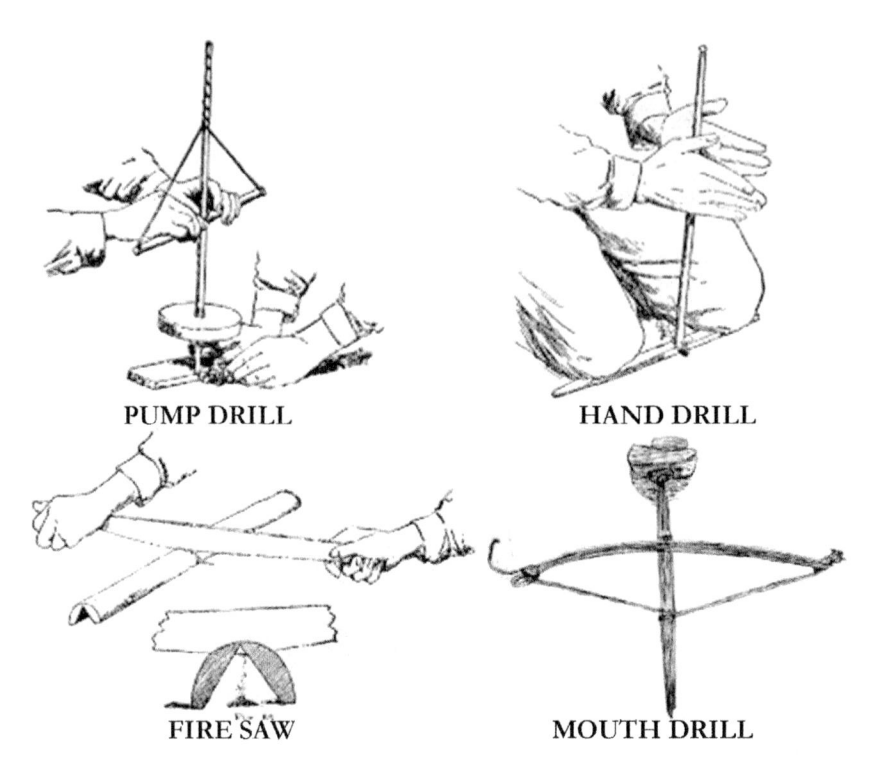

PUMP DRILL

HAND DRILL

FIRE SAW

MOUTH DRILL

TRUE NATURE

I recently learned a new one for the list from my son who is a blacksmith, the traditional way of lighting the forge. A narrow gauge piece of metal is beaten until it is glowing red hot and then used to light the forge.

Fire Lays:

- Tipi
- Bundles
- Star Fire
- Signal fire
- Cooking with rocks
- Scout pit/ snake pit fire

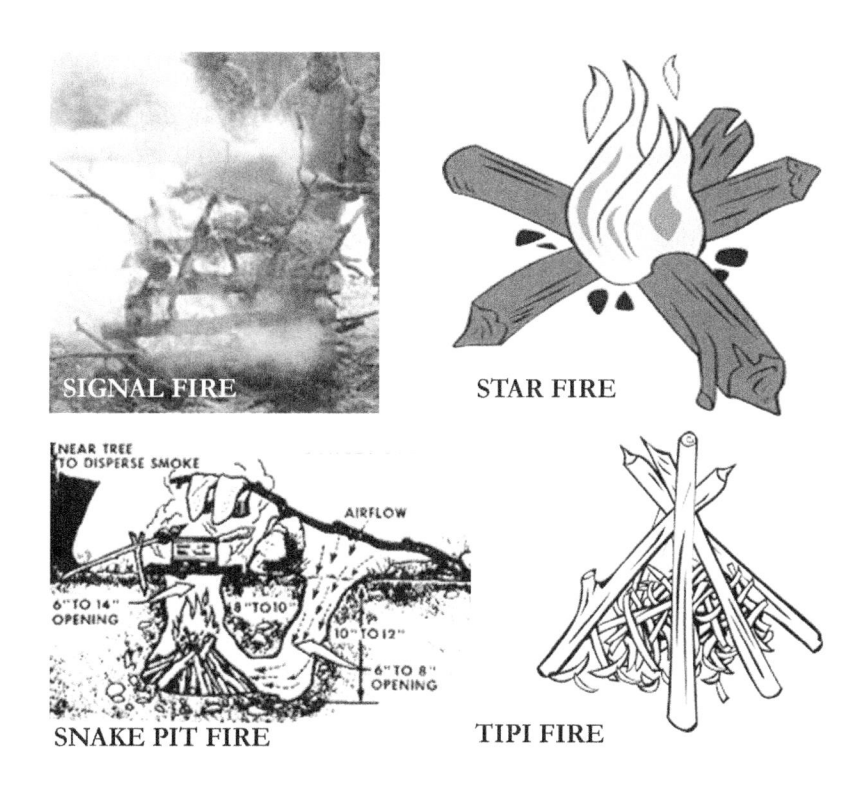

SIGNAL FIRE

STAR FIRE

SNAKE PIT FIRE

TIPI FIRE

THOMAS SCHORR-KON

THE LESSONS

The clearest lesson that fire making teaches is that of the need to make mistakes in order to learn. When we make a mistake and learn from what we did wrong we are learning, not making a mistakes. When we have made all the possible mistakes with fire making we will make it perfectly every time. We need to learn to pay attention to the detail of what we are doing. A problem only arises if we do not pay attention and repeat the same mistakes again and again.. The main principle that this brings us to is: investment in loss. Investment in loss is the notion that failure is the source of future gain. Loosing consciously develops our capacity to succeed in the future. When we learn from each attempt, knowing we are going to accomplish the task it may also become clear that whatever the problem is, is the next thing to deal with. Rather than ignoring the problem we give it our full focus.

I have also experienced the capacity of fire making to empower individuals and my favourite experience with a student started at the beginning of an introductory class. One of the students approached me as he arrived he was a big man over six feet tall and weighing in at eighteen stone. He took me aside and in a secretive tone said "I'm not a C*** or nothing but don't ask me to do anything in front of the class".

I thought about this and realised that this man had given me a gift. He was expressing his vulnerability, and was telling me of the bad experiences he had suffered at school at the hands of his teachers.

While I was in the middle of my fire making demonstration I had the opportunity to heal this deep wound. I had my hot coal in the tinder bundle and knew I was one breath away from the bundle bursting into flames. I moved over to this man and called out " Mark I have run out of puff, blow on the bundle" Instinctively he got up to blow on the bundle even after what he had said to me. It took just his one breath and the bundle burst into flames. He stood back and said "I did that" with a beaming smile on his face.

I tested him out after that to see if it had helped him get over his issues and he unflinchingly was able to hold his own in front of the group. He even returned later to complete an advanced course.

I often see the power of fire making relight some spark in people, reignite a passion, an excitement about life.

FAMILY FORAGE

We had been working all day the whole family camp gathering. First harvesting and then preparing the many wild edibles that became our feast. There were fifty of us parents and children waiting to sample the wild harvest. When I first arrived on site I had found a clutch of pheasant eggs nestled in the grass. We were in a field surrounded by oak trees, with a beautiful pond in one corner inhabited by a king fisher, with deer who wandered through from time to time. We had harvested many wild leaves for our salad, sorrel, dandelion, plantain and hawthorn topped with toasted beech and hazel nuts and coloured with red clover flowers. We had made acorn mash from the oak trees, we had reed mace (bulrushes) roots a plenty that were steamed from the ponds, we had comfrey leaves and dandelion flowers dipped in batter made with the pheasant eggs. We had burdock roots cooked in soy sauce, and shaggy parasol mushrooms. With some marinated wild venison with elderberry sauce, followed by hot wild apple and blackberry. As we gathered on the late August evening I felt the approach of a presence, a native American elder, the feeling I had was that it was my teachers mentor Stalking wolf. As if the gathering of our wild supper had drawn in this presence. I felt his nod of approval which warmed my heart and we proceeded to enjoy our wild feast. Many of the children surprised themselves with how good the food was, having expected a lean harvest from the surrounding fields.

FOOD

EDIBLE PLANTS

As we move through the year we encounter an abundance of flora to forage and preserve, there is always an abundance of something. This means more of one or two species than we could possibly collect or consume at any one time. When we were in tune with the seasons this natural cycle of collection and preservation would have been continuous. This would have been both food and medicine orientated as many plants are both edible and have multiple medicinal uses. Sometimes when we over consume certain plants we discover the power of their medicinal qualities. I remember sitting on the downs with a group of students talking to them about Plantain (Plantago Major) whilst eating seven or eight mature leaves until my tongue went numb making it tricky to talk for a short period.

Plants can be a door way to connecting with spirit, through their medicinal properties and we can develop relationships with them that go well beyond their capacity to satiate our hunger.

I remember when I visited my Aunt and Uncle in their home in the South of Italy wandering the 'Machia', (the wild areas around their old sheep farm) with my Aunt Patience Grey, she sang to the plants as we went collecting wild herbs for that days cooking.

With wild foods there are really two category's, the first eloquently coined by Crocodile Dundee are food that 'Tastes like s**t but you can live on it' and then there are gourmet foods found in the wild. What follows is a list of some of the most widely available wild plants in the U.K. they can also be found in Europe and many in North America.

SPRING EDIBLES

In the spring there is an abundance of flowers, new shoots and young leaves to eat followed by roots, fruits, nuts and seeds later in the year.

Primrose flowers (It is said you will see fairies all year if you eat the first primrose you see in the New Year)

Violets (flowers)

Rose petals (Rose hips in autumn)

Dandelion flowers and leaves (root in the autumn) Root cooked in the autumn and roasted to make a coffee substitute.

Clover: leaves and flowers, red clover is sweeter.

Gorse flowers

Sheep sorrel and wood sorrel (in small amounts as the oxalic acid inhibits the adsorption of calcium.)

Nettles, (need to be cooked) and seeds can be eaten later in the year

Shepheard's purse (Quite peppery)

Plantain (plantago major) leaves and later seeds also (Plantago lanciolata) (Leaves only)

Yarrow (small amounts)

Chick weed (small amounts as it can provoke diarrhoea)

Ground elder (cooked)

Ground Ivy (cooked)

Garlic mustard also known as Jack by the hedge

Fat hen leaves (Chenapodium) seeds can be eaten later in the year (known as goosefoot related to Quinoa)

Wild garlic (whole plant including flowers)

Dock leaves (wilted over the fire, crispy and yum) Seeds in summer, Root cooked in the autumn boil and change the water or roast.

Land cress

Colts foot leaves and flowers roast the leaves to create a salty tasting ash.

Comfrey leaves small amounts as high in Alkaloids, good dipped in batter and fried. I have recently been making falafels with them and other wild leaves.

Thistle stems (as long as they don't exude a milky sap) Root cooked in the autumn/ winter

Alexanders stem and leaves best cooked in spring.

Fresh beech leaves before they turn dark green. Nut in autumn

Hawthorne leaves I find them to be edible throughout the year. Berries in autumn can be made into fruit leather.

English Lime tree leaves

Bramble tops, (only the freshest leaves) Later blackberries

Elder flower and later Elder berries flowers dipped in batter and fried.

Pine new cone growth and pollen (as a thickener) Pine nuts later and inner bark/ rootlets all year round. Need boiling and change of water.

Reed Mace shoots also roots and rhizomes (new growth) steam or separate the starch and make into flour.

Water cress

Mint

Pig nut (root) eat fresh (looks like a chick pea)

Birch and Maple tree sap extracted can be boiled down into syrup

Fern fiddle heads/ needs boiling and then roasting. (contains five toxic principles)

Sea weeds: Samphire, Irish moss, kelp, Dulse, Nori/ larverbread, Sea lettuce and others.

LATER IN THE YEAR

Wild thyme, Wild marjoram, Wild oregano, Wild Carrot

Anjelica stems

Burdock root (cooked)

Bistort root (very hot also called water pepper)

Bugle root

Silverweed root

Lesser celandine root

Evening primrose root (boiled in several changes of water)

Acorns (boiled in several changes of water) and Oak inner bark

Birch inner bark (boiled in several changes of water)

Sweet Chestnut, Nut and inner bark (boiled in several changes of water)

Pine nut (almost a complete protein)

Beech nut. Inner bark (boiled in several changes of water)

Hazel nut. Inner bark (boiled in several changes of water)

Walnuts

Grass seeds winnow and grind for flour and roots can be roasted. The leaves can be chewed up and the juice consumed as long as the cellulose is spat out. (Wheat grass juice is highly nutritious)

Sumac flowers Used as a seasoning in Turkey makes a good drink infused in water for a few hours.

Rowan berries good for Jelly.

Yew berries taste like strawberry jam but do not eat the seed in side.

Damsons, Crab apples and other autumnal fruits

Red currants, Wild strawberries, Wild blueberries, Wild raspberries

Wild grapes and Vine leaves (boiled)

Birch twigs infused as a savoury tea stimulating.

Pine needles infused as a tea high in antioxidants fifty times stronger than vitamin C. (Picnagenol)

There are also a number of mushrooms that are safe to eat. Within the bracket fungus group none are poisonous, some are inedible and some are delicious. Oyster mushrooms, beefsteak fungus, Jews ear and chicken of the woods. Be aware that if you feel strange after eating chicken of the woods, with and slight throat constriction and strange body sensations this is because fifteen percent of people are allergic to it and the effects build up to possibly fatal after eating it 3-4 times.

The other group of mushrooms are Boletus these have a spongy surface instead of gills like pores. The poisonous varieties have red or orange pores or are bitter. Also the ones with yellow pores that turn blue when touched are also inedible.

If you want to eat mushrooms with gills then you need to study them extremely carefully as they contain specimens that are deadly poisonous.

Many insects are edible though cooking is advised to kill any parasites that might be living on them. Wood lice, worms, crickets etc I have fed these to Carol Thatcher on the Paul O'Grady show many years ago, when Carol won the" I'm a celebrity get me out of here".

I have also tried crickets whilst on an organic farm I ate a few and found them to be crunchy but sweet tasting. I was witnessed by a group of young children who a few hours later approached me with a jar full of crickets they had caught, saying "Mister do you want to eat some more" I think they wanted to watch me eat them, I politely declined as I had just had my lunch.

I have eaten butterfly Larvie called 'Suri' in the Amazon roasted in the fire, they are a major source of protein there. They taste somewhere between a pork scratching and a cheese puff, they were delicious.

Also coconut needs a mention if you are in a tropical climate as it has many phases starting as a liquid which is extremely nutritious and hydrating. Then the jelly layer forms into fat that can be used to cook with, this is sold as coconut crème, then as time passes the fat solidifies into the nut. It is possible to live on it almost exclusively. I learned about coconuts multifaceted use when I spent time on a Philippine island an hour's boat ride from the far end of Mindoro. The island belonged to a German called Frederick and I was staying there with my family and an old family friend many years ago. We would take a boat once a week to the mainland to get supplies it was a tropical island paradise.

Carob beans grow wild in the Middle East and are also an excellent food source as are dates.

THE LESSONS

AMBER AND THE BURDOCK

Using the medicinal qualities of plants can connect us more deeply with them and has the capacity to open a deeper level of connection even to the spirit of the plants.

It was a really hot day and Amber my daughter and I were playing together just enjoying each other's company. At one point Amber turned to me and filled with the joy of the moment let me know that she was happy to be with me without her mother there. This was a deeply moving moment for me as I was looking after her half of the time having separated from her mother two years before. It was moments after this that a bee came past and stung her on the thumb. She went from joy to hysteria in less than sixty seconds. I was stunned too as it felt like the beauty of the moment was shattered by the venom of this tiny bee. We moved down the hill to our camp and as we went I remembered that the day before while in the woods harvesting some 'green' Ash for working with my pole lathe, I had come upon a patch of Burdock. "Ah a healing plant to harvest for when we need it, I think it is good for stings" I thought and collected some leaves asking the plant politely. I had dried them out on the dash board of my car and as we came down the hill I suddenly realised that they were good for bee stings. I checked with my herbal and It suggested chewing up the leaves to put on. So began the task of chewing and rehydrating the Burdock leaf.

Burdock is a very bitter leaf, they can be eaten when very young but very quickly become bitter. These were not young leaves. So I began chewing making all kinds of sour faces. Then I put my chewing's on Amber's thumb. The first dollop of green pulp fell straight off. So I began to chew another leaf. Similar sour faces and much chewing later, the same thing unfortunately happened again and the precious dollop ended up on the ground for the second time. "Third time lucky?" I thought, while chomping on another Burdock leaf. This time I wrapped the chewed pulp in a whetted leaf and carefully wrapped it round her thumb. Inside a minute her whole countenance changed she forgot about the sting and went back to playing. It was at this point that a wave of thankfulness came over me, for the Burdock plant. I had been instructed to give thanks when harvesting wild plants and up till that point had done so just in word. From then on I meant it, I was actually on my hands and knees giving thanks to the burdock plant.

REVERSE CULTURE SHOCK

After the transformational experience of the first class I took with Tom Brown JR, feeling at the end of the class like at last I was no longer an alien on planet Earth. I felt like I lived here, I felt connected, like I could live anywhere on the Earth, finding all the necessities of life. I felt the connection through the tracks with all that moved on the earth. I had begun to get to know the plants as food and medicine. My view of trees had become one of awe at the many things they provided all year round. I had created wild fire a long cherished ambition. I felt alive to aspects of awareness that I had only read about in books before.

I could also see the long journey ahead the many things I did not know, things that had only been hinted at or covered in insufficient depth to have a working knowledge of due to lack of time. I felt almost overwhelmed by the mountain of information and experience that I lacked. Little did I know how much time I would spend expanding on this intense beginning. Over the years many layers of lessons began to unfold that were compressed into the first week, uncovering the underlying teachings that I sensed beneath each physical skill. Then practicing and sharing these skills with many other people.

All of this left me totally unprepared for the reverse culture shock I was just entering. From this place of total connection I returned to Grand central station 42nd street New York. I felt like the inter connectivity I had been feeling the closeness to the plants and animals was being ripped from me. I felt dislocated, alone amongst the six million inhabitants of New York City. I even felt grief stricken at this separation cast out of the "Garden of Eden". My new awareness made me raw and open, I felt under attack by the intensity of my senses. It took me two years until I finally managed to integrate this reverse culture shock.

In the intervening years my life had turned upside down. I left the inner city where I lived, broke the relationship with my partner, and found myself practicing to be an English native. I questioned if I had lost the plot, though I felt like I had found what I wanted to explore for the foreseeable future.

It was not until I was staying in New York after an intensive period of training and experience in the Pine Barrens that I was able to understand how to exist in both modalities. I was looking over the Hudson River as the sun set, the reflection on the water was of liquid fire. The buildings on either side of the river also shone with this reflected burning gold. I was quite taken by surprise. I had not felt the rapture of nature speak to me in the city. Yet here amongst the urban landscape it became clear that the beauty and natural life that I sought held in its embrace even the most imposing creations of human kind. All you had to do to connect to this was to look up.

CHAPTER 2

CONVERSATIONS WITH NATURE

"Our difficulty is that we have become autistic. We no longer listen to what the Earth, its landscape, its atmospheric phenomena and all its living forms, its mountains and valleys, the rain, the wind, and all the flora and fauna of the planet are telling us."

"We are talking only to ourselves. We're not talking to the rivers, we are not listening to the wind and stars. We have broken the great conversation. By breaking that conversation we have shattered the universe. All the disasters that are happening now are a consequence of that spiritual autism."

Thomas Berry

For millennia our environment was held in high esteem, largely because those living on the earth depended very directly on the area they inhabited for everything. When our survival is bound up with the natural world the level of our relationship to nature determines the quality of our survival. As we have become more industrialised the communication between humans and the earth has become more and more violent and unconscious. We rename rocks and minerals as resources we commodify everything. Declaring the earth to be inanimate is a triumph of the conquest of the wild and real.

"The way we see the world shapes the way we treat it. If a mountain is a deity, not a pile of ore; if a river is one of the veins of the land, not potential irrigation water; if a forest is a sacred grove, not timber; if other species are biological kin, not resources; or if the planet is our mother, not an opportunity – then we will treat each other with greater respect."   David Suzuki

Einstein's simple equation that shows that matter is bound energy has moved us away from the Newtonian clockwork view of the universe. The continued exploration of how energy is affected by consciousness with it being shown that at a subatomic level observation changes the outcome of certain experiments. Helps us understand that how we conceive of our universe has an effect on it. Whether we think of it as dead or alive has a huge bearing on us too. It is our choice to participate in the perpetuation of the world view of 'dead matter thinking' or to wake up to the aliveness of the universe. Nature will benignly reflect back to us which ever view we hold. The view that it is dead matter will lead to the destruction of the planet and us or the view of its aliveness will set us free from feeling alien and bring us home. This is also reflected in our economy; it has been termed the death economy by economist John Perkins because it focuses on profit over environmental and human costs.

Perkins is quick to point out that this isn't a global conspiracy: "They don't get together in secret meetings and plot to do evil…Rather, each group is individually driven by the same goal: to maximize profits regardless of the social and environmental costs. This is the system Perkins calls the death economy. "

Thankfully there are moves a foot by people like Polly Higgins to try to give the Earth legal status, to try to stop what she has termed ecocide so there is a possibility for the Earth to be protected with in the current framework.

The civilised view is that the wild aspects need to be subjugated. Even if we go back to Roman times we find the term Pagan was applied to the inhabitants of England. This word comes from the word 'Pagani' meaning uncivilised i.e. in need of cultivating.

A view that is older is that nature is made up of many other communities that all support us whether they are the animals or plant communities, the waters that bring life or the ancient stone beings. It is this view that everything is alive that allows us to have a dialogue with nature.

NATURES ALPHABET

First we must learn to bring our attention to nature to listen to her symphony and observe her vastness and majesty. It is during the listening that we might discern the first sound the beginning of a natural alphabet. Once we can apprehend the letters and sounds we can perhaps understand the way that nature communicates and how to communicate back with nature.

When we look into the meaning of the actual letters of the alphabet from the Phoenician and Hebrew letters that are the origin of our alphabet, we find the individual letters relate to aspects that are simple and accessible within the environment such as:

Body parts eye; tooth, open hand, fist, mouth, ear, head. Animals; ox, camel, fish. Features of nature; water, springs (the same as eye), branch of a tree, (the same as door). Other objects; House, (Temple), bowl/plate (the same as open hand), knot, door, hook or peg, fish hook.

Runes the ancient Norse script have meanings that are similarly nature related. They express natural aspects that occur within the environment they come from, with the inclusion of several deities as well:

 Animals; Domestic cattle, horse, wild ox (Auroch), Beings: humans, giant, (Thor), Ancestral God, (Odin), Other objects; Wagon, Torch, gift, cup, ancestral property, shield, Nature; Water, hail, ice, harvest, yew tree, birch tree, elk, the sun, the Earth, dawn.

There is also the Ogham a whole alphabet based on trees that was used by the Celtic Druidic tradition. As we look east we also find that Chinese and Japanese languages are based on characters representing simple natural aspects.

What this tells us is that our language even in its abstract form is grounded in nature and is derived from naturel elements. How could we have come so far from these humble beginnings, forgetting that our communication involves and is intrinsically connected to Nature.

THE MEANING OF ABC

The Phoenician alphabet differs from the Hebrew only in the symbol of each letter being drawn differently. The sounds and order are the same and when we look at the meanings of each letter we uncover an interesting insight into those ancient cultures.

If we were now to be determining a new alphabet with each letter representing a different object or aspect of our world what would we put as the first letter. I suggest that we would put the most important element first and the subsequent elements would be placed in order of importance.

If we follow this line of thinking and we unpack the meanings of ABC or the first three letters of the alphabet we find that the first letter means ox. What this indicates is that the culture identifies ox as the most important element as it can assist with tilling the soil and as in many land based cultures is a direct recognition of wealth. Farming creates surplus which leads to trade and eventually to some abstracted bartering system that eventually produces money. This abstraction draws us away from nature and the land and changes our conversation with Nature. Farming also requires a distinction of land boundaries rather than the free roaming of herd animals. The story of Cain and Abel records the first killing of one brother by another over this very issue and may well have been written around the time of the development of the Hebrew language.

The second letter means house or temple; this suggests a fixed dwelling place as opposed to a movable camp. With the notion of a house also being a place of worship we substitute our spiritual relationship with nature for worship within a small defined space. This serves to contain our rapturous wonder and reverie to a single location.

The third letter means camel; camels are both a herder's animal and an animal used for travel and trade. What we can extrapolate from this is that culturally herder's and traders were not considered as important as those farming the land. Yet most herder's would have continued at least to some degree to follow nature and therefore to be conversant with the language of nature. They would move from one pasture to another during different times of year or travel large distances navigating over vast areas of uninterrupted nature.

The shift from being followers of nature as hunters and gatherers are, to becoming farmers and creating land boundaries has reduced the need for a conversation with nature, it has altered the conversation and began a cascading effect that we are subject to today.

THE BEGINNING OF TIME

The calendar itself provides a map of our seasonal connection. By following cycles of the moon and the four main points of the solar year, the two solstices and equinoxes we can orientate ourselves with the seasonal changes and we can connect to the ancient solar celebrations that underpin the various Abrahamic religious celebrations which have been placed over these times: Interestingly the Jewish and Islamic calendars follow the lunar cycle. The term 'Movable feast' comes from the celebrations that are not on a specific day, that are set by the interface between the solar and lunar calendars. For example Easter; is calculated in accordance with the Jewish lunar calendar and then set with in the Gregorian solar calendar. The celebration of Easter is set on the first Sunday after the Passover full moon, that falls after the vernal equinox. This is the interaction of the Jewish lunar calendar and the Christian solar calendar.

The history of the calendar shows us how natural observation and connection to nature underpin our orientation through time. Initially one considers that the first people would have relied on specific natural events to determine the passage of years, the sprouting of certain plants in spring, the harvest, the migration of species etc. These observations in conjunction to the cycle of the moon provide the basis for many original calendars. Yet if the moon cycles are followed solely the calendar drifts in relation to the solar year righting itself every 33 years if no extra days are added like the current Islamic calendar.

The Mayans had a very accurate calendar for their time with their civil calendar the 'Haab' running to 365 days over 5000 years ago. Their system involved 3 calendars The 'Tzolkin' or sacred calendar with 260 days interlocking with the 'Haab' every 52 years and their long count lasting for around 7885 solar years.

The Egyptians calendar was based around the annual Nile floods that occurred just after the appearance of the star Sirius on the horizon, again their calendar had 365 days at around 4236 BCE. They had 12 months with 30 days and added 5 days of celebration to complete the number of days.

The Chinese calendar had 354 days around 2637 BCE and was a lunar calendar. Most of the lunar calendars were based on a 19 year period with 7 years having 13 months, each month containing 29 ½ days. This included the Chinese, Babylonians, Greeks and Jews. This was also used by the Arabs until Muhammed forbade the shift from 12 to 13 months. The 19 year cycle would be out in relation to solar years by one week per 19 years.

Calendar is a Roman word and theirs had 304 days this was remedied in 700CE to 355 days with the addition of an extra month of 22-23 days every 2 years. Then Cesar changed it in 45 BCE by adding 80 days and then using 365 ¼ days. He also moved the start of the year from the vernal equinox to the first of January. I like to think that it was his association with Cleopatra and the Egyptian calendar that brought about this change.

Pope Gregory reformed the calendar in 1582 to 365 days 5 hours 49 mins and 12 seconds

There are various archaeological finds such as Warrens field that show European monumental lunar calendars in use at least 8000-10,000 years ago, 5000 years before Mesopotamian calendars which are some of the oldest. Interestingly warrens field is also aligned to the winter solstice as well as the lunar months. Similarly Stonehenge oriented towards the summer solstice and around 5000 years old and Newgrange in Ireland orientated to the winter solstice and around 5200 years old. These are relics that point to a sophisticated understanding of the passage of time that our ancestors would have known, a way of relating to the natural cycles a conversation with both terrestrial and celestial nature. This knowledge would have been key to survival whether people were hunter gatherers or herders or farmers, it is only in the industrialised age that we can live in a disconnected way from these natural cycles.

Our relationship to the passing of time can either connect us to the natural cycles bringing us into a relationship with natural time and the vast celestial movements that create the rhythm which affect our lives or it can isolate us and give us a great deal of anxiety and even make us seriously ill. Larry Dossey in his 1982 book 'Space, Time and Medicine,' concluded that people caught up in time battling had stress related illnesses that range from nervous exhaustion to heart disease and form a pathological condition he called "time-sickness".

Larry Dossey found that using biofeedback treatments that help regulate brainwave function can solve many of the stress related issues people caught up in the work treadmill succumb to. The same brainwave regulation can be achieved through Meditation, Tai Chi, and other simple interventions including moving more slowly in a natural way, slowing the breath thus tuning us into the natural rhythms that our brain and body are more allied to.

As a follower of nature myself there are certain timings that I notice, certain moments or synchronised natural aspects that integrate with the calendar. There are some that have been recognised for centuries such as St John's wort, a beautiful healing plant that flowers on St John's day just after the summer solstice. One of its uses is for depression as it flowers at the height of the solar year. Lilly of the valley flowers in early spring around the equinox and is a symbol of Easter especially in France. If we are paying attention we notice the beautiful procession of plants and trees from the first flowering of the black thorn in the spring hedge rows through such delightful events like the release of thistle down on to the wind in early August. It could be that we are more tuned to the birds and await the song of the nightingale to tell us of the return of spring or on hearing the chiffchaff we become alert to the return of sunny days. It could be that we start to get cosy as the swallows return to warmer climates. There are a multiplicity of natural indicators of the seasonal change some more noticeable than others.

This is not a recommendation to follow some kind of superstition it is about listening to and reconnecting with the natural cycles in the face of a 24/7 culture that tries to overcome seasonality by making everything available at all times. With a race to deliver immediately and where time off is regulated by the superimposition of particular belief structures, over key moments in natural time. Rather than the simplicity of acknowledging those moments in the flow of the cycle. Where being busy is seen as a badge of honour and taking time off is seen as laziness.

There are however still a few historic examples of our natural relationship to the seasons one is still present in the long summer holidays in the school calendar which are a leftover from a time when children would help with the harvest.

We currently hold the view that time is money a quote often attributed to Benjamin Franklin. It may have originated from an interesting practice that was much used in England that of setting a pocket watch by the clock at Greenwich and then selling the time to businesses in London this practice was carried out by one particular family and continued into the 20th century.

A more life affirming view is that time is sacred and your time here is sacred to you.

Marking these major moments in natural time have become the basis for many religions, the moments symbolised in different ways. This started with the 'worshiping' of the sun. Yet the observance of these times of year only have personal meaning if we either join together with people who share our view point at these times or if we have a valid way of expressing ourselves, a valid way of communicating with nature, celebrating and praying to spirit.

With an awareness of the celestial rhythms we may still feel the lack of proximity of these grand celestial events. Where a level of local nature communication is available, on a daily basis, we can feel part of the greater conversation. It is through our everyday connection that we gain an understanding of how nature communicates with us.

WEEKLY PLANETS

Every week we journey through the solar system. looking at the days of the week we are exposed to a lesson in the celestial bodies known in classical times. The planets that were known at this time were the sun, the moon, Mars, Mercury, Jupiter, Venus and Saturn. If we take both English and French together we get the full planetary list;

Sunday, Sun, Monday, Moon, *Mardi*, Mars, *Mercredi*, Mercury, *Jeudi*, Jupiter, *Vendredi*, Venus, Saturday, Saturn.

The Anglo-Saxons replaced the four Norse gods Tiw, Woden, Thor and Frigg, to make Tuesday, Wednesday, Thursday and Friday.

We all love to watch nature programs that reveal the secret life of nature, yet we are still so disconnected from these secret goings on around where we live. Tracking is a vital alphabet of nature that tantalises us with mysteries to unravel in our search for understanding. A primal alphabet of the movement of the earth showing us the intricacies of the other lives that interweave with our own. The movement and calls of birds and animals similarly offer us clues as to what is going on. The flow of wind and clouds, tell us about the changes in weather. The growth of plants, the changing seasons and the phases of the moon inform us of the larger movements inherent in nature. Similarly the turning of the constellations spells out the movement of the year. All of these languages key us into some aspect of listening to nature and help us to understand how to communicate.

THOMAS SCHORR-KON

THE SCIENCE OF OMENS

The first omens were recorded in ancient Mesopotamia some 5200 years ago. Interestingly they studied as many aspects and phenomena as possible to incorporate into their study of omens, from celestial bodies to natural happenings and also many unnatural types of events e.g. seeing a large beast with birds feet. This curiosity and categorising of so many phenomena is considered to be the beginning of Science.

"When every single phenomenon in the world could be considered as a possible object for recording in the spirit of examination and divinatory deduction, one can see in this attitude an early example of encyclopaedic curiosity, which is the basis for all scientific endeavour. (Bottero 1992:127)"
Amar Annus 2009 Divination and the interpretation of signs in the ancient world. P2.

The view that any aspect of the natural world could speak to us as an omen may well have been held for a very long time before this, yet it was committed to writing only a millennium after writing was invented and was elucidated in great detail in the Babylonian Diviner's Manual

(Enuma anu Enlil)

"The omens and other lore of the Mesopotamian scholars represented divine wisdom that ideologically originated in primeval times of the antediluvian period, but which was being continuously updated and outlined by the scientific methods of the day."
Amar Annus 2009 Divination and the interpretation of signs in the ancient world. P3

Another side issue is how these Mesopotamian omens from their extensive texts appear in the New Testament (Amar Annus P5-6 gives various examples).
I am not suggesting a return to pre-Abrahamic interpretations of phenomena what we would today associate more with superstition, I am merely trying to bring our attention to the natural world as a source of feedback, information and the possibly of conversation. We have for millennia studied natural phenomena and in our post-industrial condition we closed ourselves of to this information.

TRUE NATURE

I find the history of a particular pursuit tells us a lot about how it is unconsciously driven.

The idea that science has come from the study of phenomena to predict out comes and that in the first instance they were omens is what this points to. Science generally seeks to disprove theories it does produce information that helps us understand phenomena and predict outcomes.

Embedded within our weather obsessed nation there is a rich culture of folk sayings mostly attributed to sailors and shepherds, that we are most probably familiar with these are weather omens. There are various different phenomena that if we pay attention to we can read what is going to happen, from clouds, wind direction, the flight of birds, animal behaviour, trees and plants, lunar activity and more.

Here are various weather predictors that you might know or find useful to know:

SKY AND CLOUDS

Perhaps the most familiar weather predictions are "Red sky at night Shepheard's delight"
What this is telling you is that in the west where the sun is setting there is a high pressure system stirring dust into the atmosphere, and as the main prevailing wind in the northern hemisphere is south west this will be coming towards you. Similarly the opposite is true and the accompanying rhyme is: "A red sky in the morning shepherds warning ". The dry air has now passed you and rain will follow.
Similarly a rainbow in the east means the rain has left the area and a rainbow in the west means the rain is heading towards you.

Cloud formations can tell us a lot about weather conditions the most useful rhyme is "Mares tails and mackerel scales, tall ships carry short sails." This means rain will follow the next day after these cloud formations which usually occur in a fairly clear warm sky signalling a change of weather.

TIMING

Another one that always seems to work is, rain before seven dry by eleven.

Dew before midnight, the next day is sure to be bright.

I personally find that two things occur just before rain falls firstly the birds quieten down and secondly there is a strong gust of wind a minute or so before it rains. The birds will also start singing again once the rain has stopped.

LUNAR CHANGES

If there is a ring around the moon at night, snow or rain will come in the next 3 days, I was not sure about this one but as I write there is snow on the ground 2 days after seeing a ring around the moon.

I have also found that the weather will change to its opposite just after the full moon.

PLANT INDICATIONS

Flowers are said to smell stronger than normal when rain is on its way.

Oak before ash in for a splash or Ash before Oak in for a soak, These signs tell us what will happen longer into the future, they indicate whether there will be a wet or dry summer.

BIRD INDICATIONS

Birds that feed on insects like swallows and swifts will be seen to be flying high when there is high pressure as the insects float higher and if they are flying lower there is low pressure so expect rain.

WIND DIRECTION

It is worth being aware of the wind direction as different types of weather are blown towards us from the different directions. For example a north wind will bring much colder weather.

ANIMAL INDICATIONS

Before the devastating tsunamis in Asia animals suddenly rushed to higher ground and away from the ocean, People who saw them and decided to follow survived

REPTILES

Snakes seem to be especially sensitive to earthquakes.

Frogs and toads croak louder and longer before rain.

Frogs singing in the evening means fair weather the next day.

KING SOLOMON

THE FIRST RECORDED NATURALIST

King Solomon was reputed to have been taught the speech of birds and had great knowledge of the plants and trees. He supposedly chose to be able to understand the birds and animals instead of seeking wealth or being able to subjugate his enemies.

The Qur'an states that Solomon was "taught the speech of birds." (See Qur'an Chapter 27, Verses 15-20)

'He spoke about plant life, from the cedar of Lebanon to the hyssop that grows out of walls. He also spoke about animals and birds, reptiles and fish.' 1 kings 4:33

There are quite a few theories and speculation about the meaning of Solomon being able to understand the language of birds, whether he communicated by sending carrier pigeons or could read hieroglyphics as the symbols contain many birds. Yet judging by how he was held in such high esteem and his naturalist knowledge was broad I suggest that he may well have understood one of the languages of nature that of bird communication.

St Frances of Assisi much later was similarly endowed with this capacity. He also eschewed wealth and perhaps this lack of materialism or unencumbered simple living is bound up with this level of connection.

In Africa there is one species of bird that is in direct communication with humans this is the honey guide. A recent scientific study by evolutionary biologist Claire Spottiswoode demonstrated that reciprocal signaling between the honey guides and humans is definitely going on. This is a long standing relationship of humans calling the honey guides and them responding, then leading the humans to a hive so the humans can get the honey and leave the bird to feast on the wax. This is a very concrete and very specific example of communicating with nature.

Ravens the most intelligent of birds clocking up the largest number of calls for any species, have also been known to lead wolves and hunters to elk, caribou herds and seals. Known to interact with wolves and to feed on hunted carcasses, they have even been observed playing with young wolf cubs to establish a bond. Inuit hunters were aware of their communications and if they circled and called would follow and be led to good hunting opportunities. I have read accounts of them trying to wake sleeping bears when salmon are swimming nearby to get the dozing bears to go fishing so they can get some scraps. (Mind of the raven Bernd Heinrich) This is another example of birds communicating directly with humans and other animals.

In many earth connected cultures there is an understanding of listening to the communications of birds, their alarm calls and their flight patterns to gain vital information about what is going on in the environment. It is as if the birds are an aspect of the voice of nature and listening and observing their behaviour gives us a way to join the conversation. The flight of a water bird in an arid area will indicate the direction of water. The silence of birds indicates the presence of danger. The alarming or scolding calls of birds indicates the presence of predators. These observations and many more are available to us every day and key us into a deeper awareness of the natural world. Similarly the level to which we leave them undisturbed or disrupt these goings on tells us directly how tuned in we are at any given moment. Apache scouts are credited with being able to tell from their understanding of bird language the approach of non-scouts from up to two miles away.

In our woodland environment we usually get at least a two minute warning.

HUMANS BEST FRIEND

Humans have had relationships with animals since they began, humans are animals, so we have an innate capacity to connect to and communicate with our world. Before the domestication of animals we can only guess as to our capacity to communicate. Yet if primitive cultures offer any clues when looking at them we realise very quickly that their careful observation of animals fuelled by their hunting needs gave them a very acute knowledge of the animals they live close to. Dogs were domesticated some 15,000 years ago sheep 13,000-11,000, cattle some 10,500 years ago and horses 6000-4000 years ago, cats by the Egyptians 4000 years ago. So even if we are looking at historical capacity to communicate with nature we have been cultivating close relationships with certain animals for quite a while. In Scandinavian countries there are particular songs sung, hauntingly high pitched to bring the cattle to the singer this is called Kulning it has similarities to Yodeling. This practice of Kulning is very old and is considered a Viking legacy.

Certain Adivasi tribes (India's native tribes) still today pay a young boy to enter the forest and befriend the wild cattle giving them salt, which they craved, over time enticing them into the village, this might be similar to how cattle were domesticated originally.

WHAT DOES THIS MEAN

While we may be able to communicate with specific animals and have developed longstanding mutually beneficial relationships with certain species what of all the other wilder animals that we might encounter in what seem like a random manner. Is there any significance to us encountering a fox or a deer, perhaps we just keep seeing squirrels or butterflies, maybe we regularly hear the call of owls or see them roosting in the day. Whatever the encounter do we consider this a communication from nature? And if this is a communication from nature what does it mean?

We may be familiar with the concept that the type of energy we put out we attract. Well this is very evident in nature. We meet a dog and suddenly feel fearful of its size etc.. the dog reacts by barking and expresses our fear back to us. On the other hand when we show affection the animal responds accordingly. Unless it's benign nature has been changed to malignant by training or abuse.

When we see an animal it is communicating something to us, it could be a seasonal communication, a personal communication, a warning like an omen, or some kind of sign. It is as if the physical appearance becomes a metaphor. How we interpret theses metaphors depends on several things. Largely the symbolic qualities of an animal are derived directly from its physical characteristics, though there are some cultural differences that might need to be taken into consideration. Then there is our own catalogue of previous experiences which might hone the experience to some more specific meaning to us.
Animals behaving strangely might also draw specific attention and meaning.
Fox and Badger are good examples of how physical characteristics translate directly into meanings. Fox immediately brings up notions of sly movement and camouflage and we find this borne out in its way of moving, to give a simple example; with in the dog family it is the only member that moves more like a cat, not showing its claws and its rear feet stepping directly into the track left by the front (a direct register). Badger is considered aggressive and tenacious and we find that unlike most animals its lower jaw is physically held by the bones of the skull meaning if it latches on it has a much greater power to hold on and not let go.
Cultural differences are apparent in the interpretation of owl. The Native North American view is that of it representing supernatural forces at work, while in the European tradition Owl has more of a reputation for wisdom.

It is also possible for the communication from nature to be far more direct.

TRUE NATURE

MIK MAK CHIEF AND THE BEAR

I heard a story from a Mick Mack chief from Newfoundland. He had been invited to Bristol to hold a council at the time of the 500 year anniversary of the sailing of the Mathew to Newfoundland by John Cabot from Bristol. The ship had been lovingly recreated and was going to retrace the journey. The rebuilding of the boat was exquisite but it was an extremely culturally insensitive act to sail it back across to Newfoundland. So a number of Bristol inhabitants rallied to show support for the tribal peoples who were affected by this. The main organiser was later invited to Newfoundland and on her return told me this story about the chief.

He had built a cabin on tribal lands in the distant forest. Having completed the work he came back to where he lived. Several months passed and he returned to the cabin only to find a bear had broken into the cabin and smashed it up. Thinking that the bear lived there too he rebuilt the cabin stayed a while and then came back. On his next visit he found a bear had done the same thing smashing the place up. He made the repairs and then started to make a 'settlers welcome mat' this is a wooden board with nails sticking up through, like a small bed of nails; it is put inside the door so if a bear comes in it does not return. Half way through making this he decided he could not go through with it, instead he wrote a note in Mick Mack and pinned it to the door. It read 'Dear bear take what you like but leave the place in good order'

He left to return again several months later. On his return he found the place in good order the only thing he noticed was that the water butt had a large bear clawed gash in it. So he declared to my friend, "All the animals around here speak Mick Mack".

Within certain Adivasi tribes in India the view held by the people was that the domesticated animals in their compound were under their jurisdiction. The animals that lived in the wild areas were under the guiding hand of the spirits of the uncultivated areas. With this view the hunters had to communicate with the guardian spirits of the wild areas in order to ask if they could take one of their herd. Because of the hunters need to develop this level of communication they often became the shamans as they got more experienced.

One route to develop a close relationship with the animals is through the science and art of tracking we are invited into understanding their physical characteristics and ways. It is from this that we extrapolate the meaning of our encounters with them through the third sacred question "what does this mean?" In this way the physical aspects can be seen as the metaphor for us to be able to understand the meaning from.

PLANT COMMUNICATION

We now know scientifically that plants respond to being touched, and can communicate to each other through an underground fungal network thanks to the work of Paul Stamets through what is now being called "the wood wide web".

"Suzanne Simard demonstrated in 1997 how different species of trees are able to exchange carbon by means of mycelia, she used paper birch and Douglas fir in her research. Simard's research shows that larger trees help younger trees, especially saplings growing in the shade, by sharing carbon. Plants can even hear when they are being eaten and release chemicals to try to stop their leaves being devoured. "

Appel,H.M. & Cocroft, R.B. Oecologia (2014

When plants are touched different sensations trigger a cascade of physiological and genetic changes that depend on the stimulation the plants are getting, whether it's a few drops of rain, or a gentle touch.

"Although people generally assume plants don't feel when they are being touched, this shows that they are actually very sensitive to it," lead researcher Oliver Van Aiken

In 2010 Ren Sen Zeng of South China Agricultural University in Guangzhou showed how plants warn each other through mycelial connections of impending attack by blight causing fungi. Also David

Johnson of the University of Aberdeen showed in 2013 how broad beans warned each other of the impending approach of aphids through similar mycelial communications.

There is some evidence to suggest that plants respond to direct communication as plants need to be able to respond to various types of stimulus in order to survive for example plants exposed to wind produce a growth retardant hormone to make their stems shorter and thicker.

"Jagadis Bose, who developed some of the earliest work on plant neurobiology in the early 1900s, treated plants with a wide variety of chemicals to see what would happen. In one instance, he covered large, mature trees with a tent then chloroformed them. (The plants breathed in the chloroform through their stomata, just as they would normally breathe in air.) Once anesthetized, the trees could be uprooted and moved without going into shock. He found that morphine had the same effects on plants as that of humans, reducing the plant pulse proportionally to the dose given. Too much took the plant to the point of death, but the administration of atropine, as it would in humans, revived it. Alcohol, he found, did indeed get a plant drunk. It, as in us, induced a state of high excitation early on but as intake progressed the plant began to get depressed, and with too much it passed out. and it had a hangover the next day Irrespective of the chemical he used, Bose found that the plant responded identically to the human; the chemicals had the same effect on the plants nervous systems as it did the human. This really should not be surprising. The neurochemicals in our bodies were used in every life-form on the planet long before we showed up. They predate the emergence of the human species by hundreds of millions of years. They must have been doing something all that time, you know, besides waiting for us to appear."
— Stephen Harrod Buhner, Plant Intelligence and the Imaginal Realm: Beyond the Doors of Perception into the Dreaming of Earth

RELATIONSHIP TO NATURE

I always felt a deep connection to trees as a child but over the years I have developed a deep and respectful relationship with plants. My real journey with plants began as I discovered many wild edibles after my first class in New Jersey with Tom Brown Jr. I was living on Dartmoor and started gathering and eating weeds as I learned how to be an English native. As I started to investigate the medicinal properties of these so called weeds I found them to be extremely effective medicines, and they began to teach me about gratitude and increased my ability to rely on nature in a number of medical emergency situations. This gave me the confidence to use plants to heal my three children of most of their childhood illnesses. As I travelled I was both reassured by the presence of healing plants I knew and had the curiosity to find out about native plants and remedies of the countries I visited.

Then when I was suffering from a serious case of man flu one of the plants spoke to me and indicated that it was the plant to cure my condition. Curiosity begins the conversation which can then develop into a relationship. This relationship has the capacity to lead to the spirit of the plant or other part of nature communicating with us directly.

Paracelsus popularised the ancient idea of the doctrine of signatures. Expressing the view that the appearance of the plant and where it grows tells us a lot about the plants healing capacity suggesting that a lot of information is available to us even with our normal senses. Yet by seeking to discover for ourselves the healing qualities of a plant we are beginning a relationship directly with the plant and with nature as a whole. We are engaging in a connection with context as well as specific constituent chemicals that allows us to incorporate a concept of wholeness that includes the personality of the plant as a factor to engage with perhaps leading us to a connection with its spirit at a later date.

There is a tradition in South America that I came across during my time in the Amazon. The approach is of taking time alone in the jungle and eating a simple diet with the ingestion of a weak brew of a particular tree or pant. This is called a plant diet the outcome of this is a possible meeting with the spirit of the plant or tree. This is usually undertaken under the watch full eye of a shaman who has already undergone this rite of passage. The shaman then builds knowledge of how she/ he can use the plants for healing and creates a personal relationship with the spirit of the plants.

Even without going through this process a great deal of herbal knowledge is known by the locals. It is as if the generations of shaman that have undergone this process have been instructed to use the plants in similar ways. The sense that I picked up when I was in South America was that this process that is still practiced in Peru could well have been the source of much of the herbal knowledge that is now recorded in Europe.

Trees play a vital role in this as there spirit is altogether more accessible because of their size and presence and they offer much powerful healing that tends to be side lined with in herbal medical practice with the exception of one or two. When I teach herb lore I encourage my novice students to meditate with the spirit of the plants, to ask them what they can be used for. Then they set about looking up their qualities. The results of this exercise often surprise those participating, that the information is accessible directly from the plant.

It is important to me to develop a relationship with plants, one of respect and understanding. We may be moving too fast or have our heads too full to be still enough to hear the plants communicate with us, and it is not necessarily a dialogue that uses our spoken language. It is more the language of the heart, of feeling, intuition and imagination that for so long has been written off as a childish practice while logical scientific thinking has become the dominant modus operandi. Yet how many of us are prepared to train this part of ourselves to reach beyond the confines of our physical mind. We all have experiences that touch into this deeper knowing, though we mostly write them off as just our imagination or a coincidence.

"For the most part, these wonderful dream powers lie dormant in our society, but the Huichols and the Matsés of the Amazon consider dream learning to be true learning. Indeed, nearly every culture on earth, except our own, respects dream learning as true learning. We revere the rational, analytical method of learning that has been honed and polished since the days of the ancient Greeks. We do not realize that the shamans of our species have honed and polished another method. This dreaming method is neither rational nor analytical, but it works extremely well."

Plant Spirit Medicine by Eliot Cowan, page 9

Working with the healing virtues of plants to me is a doorway to connecting with spirit. To know that these other life forms are there willingly giving us so much healing potential always inspires my gratitude and awe.

"Plants wish us well in every way. They are perfectly willing to bring us into the blessings of their union with nature. But, as the plantain spirit told me, they can do nothing unless they are asked. I would add that we have to know the right questions and the right way to ask them."

Plant Spirit Medicine Eliot Cowan Page 17

If you were a doctor and were woken in the middle of the night bundled into the boot of a car and driven at top speed to an unknown destination, flung out and asked to perform a healing how would you feel? So imagine how a plant might feel. If we act respectfully, asking the plant, thanking it, taking time to listen to it, we may find it will guide us as well as heal our client.

"There is only one active ingredient in plant medicines: friendship. A plant spirit heals a patient as a favour to its friend-in-dreaming, the doctor."

Plant Spirit Medicine Eliot Cowan, page 4

We have been brought up to view that all life forms are in a hierarchy insects and plants at the bottom and humans up at the top. It is true that humans are quite remarkable creatures, yet by holding to this hierarchical view we serve to separate ourselves from the flow of life, we set ourselves apart.   It is this view that makes it most difficult for us to explore a real communication with plants, animals, and the whole of Nature because we view ourselves as above it.

"Somewhere along the way, we lost the experience of unity. We live our lives propping up the pathetic lie that we are different from everything else. This is a lie because the same awareness shines in the heart of all things. The lie is pathetic because it dooms us to a dry life of alienation."
Plant Spirit Medicine, Eliot Cowan

"Dualism is the proto-dream underlying clock time and all modern dreaming. Dualism might be defined as the illusion that there are two discreet principles in the universe: self and other. Dualism implies isolation, conflict, and a continuous struggle of opposing forces."
Plant Spirit Medicine by Eliot Cowan, page 35

Again imagine you are a profound healer and someone is asking for your healing assistance but is talking down to you as if you were a lesser being and you can feel that their thanks are just mouthed and not heart felt. This may influence the assistance you give.

I have had a number of experiences where plants have come to my aid either communicating with me or making themselves available before they were needed and so being on hand for emergencies.

Several years ago I was struck down by a summer flue with headache and light fever. I had been confined to bed for a couple of days and nothing I tried was working to throw of the symptoms. We were staying with some friends and were expecting guests for dinner. I had just mustered the strength to go out for a walk for the first time in several days and while walking next to the lake on my friends land saw a whole bank of Meadowsweet (*Filipendula Ulmaria*) the plant called to me indicating it was the plant I needed. So I picked a few flower heads and went back into make a brew. After one cup of tea with two flower heads in I suddenly felt human again. The headache was removed the grogginess left and my energy began to return. I rushed out to collect some more for when the effect of the first cup wore of. I was then able, with doses every few hours to help with the dinner and enjoy it too.

I later looked it up and realised that the salicylic acid must have been the main active ingredient in removing my headache and grogginess, it was also somewhat decongesting. These are not its main properties and normal use, as it is mostly used for calming the stomach and for diarrhea. I now gather meadowsweet every year to have it on hand for when it is needed.

When we connect with the plants getting to know their habitat and growing cycle we are making relations with them and as we ingest them and use them perhaps even knowing the wider context of their use beyond their medicinal value we find that wherever we go we encounter these plant friends helping us to feel more at home in nature more that we live on the earth rather than strangely separate from it.

This creates a great freedom being able to take our medicine directly from the environment around us.

EARTH MAN

The word man and human in English are derived from the Latin words *homo* and *humanus* with the word *humus* meaning earth, ground or soil.

In Hebrew the word for man is Adam the first man of the bible, the word for earth or ground in Hebrew is *adamah* and in the Bible Adam was made from the earth.

When Adam and Eve are put in the garden they are set to look after it, this is their primary purpose. So if you are lacking a purpose the Old Testament provides the first purpose for man and woman within the Abrahamic traditions.

Within the Native American traditions there is a similar concept. That all of creation was given instructions and only humans have forgotten their original instruction. Every other part of the unfoldment of nature is following its original instructions except humans.

REWILDING

Caretaking is a practice that centres on communication with nature.

The interesting outcome of this desire to communicate with the land to help to bring it back into balance, is that this strengthens our capacity to communicate with the spirit of place and therefore with spirit per say.

The collaborative practice of caretaking is one of giving back to the Earth. The Earth that has nourished us with her life's blood all the days we have been alive. Unfortunately we are living under the assumption that we are insignificant and can make no difference. The opposite is true; every part of the whole that we encourage towards balance reverberates out like a beautiful song in the darkness, able to touch the heart of the listener, inciting them to dance in tune with the wild natural world bringing balance with every step.

This could be simply expressed by the picking up of litter, or the heartfelt tending of your garden or lending your support to halt the destruction of nature to pillage some local resource.

READING'S COPSE SPRING EQUINOX BULLDOZERS AND THE CHERRY PICKER

I spent some time at the Newbury bypass protest in 1996 and witnessed a very direct communication from the Earth. It was the spring equinox and the tallest tree on the route was about to be evicted. The activists were occupying the two tree houses they had built one above the other on this immense pine tree. The security firm had brought in a cherry picker from Europe that was large enough to remove the protesters. It arrived and at full extension towered over the tree. While it flexed its crane like arm, bulldozers were busily at work pushing over ancient oaks at the base of the tree, suddenly one of the oak trees spun round as it was being bulldozed and crashed down on the control panel of the giant cherry picker stopping the eviction for the day. It felt like the earth was saying, 'Not to day you don't' as this happened on the spring equinox. Sad to say they returned the next day to finish the job.

Caretaking recognises the capacity of organisms to self-organise understanding that they can come into balance of their own accord though this might take a long time. Any intervention is thus a movement towards creating balance on the land. In the U.K. the landscape has been managed for hundreds of years and few places exhibit a balanced eco system. So the need to observe, listen and then respond to the land from a rewilding view point is paramount. Any rewilding will affect the whole, whether we are just adding a wildlife pond to the end of our garden, or growing a wildflower lawn or meadow for bats and butterflies. Permaculture principles aim to work with the land and perpetuate the idea of observing the land for a year before doing anything. This is a way of beginning a dialogue, by listening to the land.

Returning native species like bringing back beavers and replanting trees are implicated in possible solutions to reducing flooding that has been affecting many households across the country. Creating an integrated approach which includes land owners and farming traditions is key to rewilding being taken up. Farmers and land owners have been actively caretaking some times for generations.

When this caretaker's approach is applied on a larger scale it is called rewilding. A well-known example of this was the reintroduction of wolves into Yellowstone in 1995. This created a top down cascade of positive effects called a 'Tropic Cascade'. The wolves kept the elk herds moving, thus letting the willow and aspen regenerate on the river banks that were being over grazed. This helped to repair the river banks and increasing beaver numbers who feed on the willows. The wolves have also inadvertently helped feed ravens, eagles, magpies, coyotes and bears through elk carrion.

Another example is in Jorhat India where Jadav Payeng planted trees and tended them on a sand bar in the river Brahmaputra creating a forest reserve over several decades. I have also seen similar projects implemented in the Amazon to return areas of forest where it has been decimated.

The instance of native peoples to keep their lands free of resource exploitation and pollution is an expression of the original act of caretaking.

TREE PREACHING

The most direct form of communication with nature I have come across was taught to me as tree preaching by Tom Brown Jr. He told us a story of having been wrongfully accused of putting a dead mouse in the principles drawer at school and subsequently being kept in for a detention at the end of school on Friday. He would normally have high tailed it out to the woods to spend time with his Apache mentor Stalking wolf, who he called Grandfather. When he arrived before he could unburden himself of his troubles Grandfather pointed to the edge of the cedar swamp and said "tell it to the trees". Tom even more down cast did what he was instructed, and began to mumble to the majestic cedars. Not long after he had begun to mumble, grandfather called to him "PREACH it to the trees". Tom with a bit of a shock began to preach, imaging he was like a fire and brimstone preacher, sharing all his emotional troubles and then his tacking difficulties etc.. As he expressed himself with emotion to the trees he found answers coming back to him, both feeling the release of emotion and finding insight. Within the caretaking context this can be adapted to focus on receiving specific information from the land.

This approach has the capacity to help us deal with a vast array of personal issues and develops our capacity to receive insight directly from nature. In his book "The smell of rain on dust" Martine Prechtel in talking about the transformation of grief to praise elucidates how culturally we would have been held within our society, as we released the emotion and disruption that ensues as we come to terms with the death of our loved ones. Martine Prechtel acknowledges that there is no longer the cultural context for this grief to be held. Interestingly this was maintained in the U.K. in a formal way until the advent of the First World War by the Victorians having a prescribed period of mourning, wearing black etc which became untenable after the wholesale slaughter of a generation in the aftermath of the war.

Martine Prechtel expresses how our grief is an expression of the depth of our love for what or whom has passed over, and how as we express this we can transmute our grief into praise. He says 'Grief and praise are the tenants of love'.

Martine Prechtel reminds us that we are part of the Earth and that we exist within the wider community of all living things so can express our grief within the context and holding of that community.

"No matter what kind of person goes to the sea to grieve, we must have people to help us when we are in this place. Even if we are not capable of being in grief, or we think we can handle it ourselves, we need people to help us grieve as best we can even if we are not yet good at it. This is no race or competition, but a natural function, a gift from life to make life livable again, for those who would live life all the way: those who fall in love. You might expect that, after 2.000 or 3,000 years of repression and a culturally endorsed incapacity with grief, most individuals would be totally inept at letting grief roll out onto the beach to the mother of us all: the salty ocean. But it usually comes as a great surprise and relief how naturally people grieve when it is safe to do so. So we need the ocean and a friend."

Martine Prechtel the smell of rain on dust page 51

This indicates that our communication with nature our conversation has the capacity to be held at a deep and profound level. Bringing us to the recognition of the scope of nature based healing, ceremony or the more modern form of this, therapy.

Two other forms of grief that are worthy of mention here that can specifically impede us having this conversation are; grief that we hold for the destruction of the earth and anger or grief that the land can have in respect of how humankind has treated it.

Johanna Macey has developed the work that reconnects a whole body of work centred on integrating the deeply debilitating feelings of despair we can hold in respect of how the earth is being destroyed. This work seeks to develop the power and capacity to act to heal the world through the honouring of grief and bringing to awareness our interrelationship with all things.

"Drawing from deep ecology, systems theory and spiritual traditions, the Work that Reconnects (WTR) builds motivation, creativity, courage and solidarity for the transition to a sustainable human culture."

Another facet of grief is the grief that the land can hold when it has been abused and as we start our conversation with the land we may encounter this as the primary response to our conversation. Stephen Harrod Buhner recounts an experience of his, from his book "Sacred Plant Medicine":

"In this process of unlearning, in the process of feeling and hearing the plants again, one comes to realize many things. And of these things, perhaps stronger than the others, one feels the pain of the Earth. It is not possible to escape it.
One of the most powerful experiences I had of this was the year when I travelled to the Florida panhandle. One day Trishuwa and I decided to go out and make relationship with the plants and offer prayer to them. The place we chose appeared quite lush, with huge trees and thick undergrowth. But as we sat there, a strong anger came from the land and the trees. They had little use for us and told us so in strong language. We spoke with them for a long time and did not cower away from their rage and eventually, as we received their pain and anger, they calmed down a little. They told us that we could do our ceremonies if we wished and that they appreciated the thought but that it would do no good. It was too late for that place, it could not be helped, the land would take its revenge for the damage done to it and nothing would stop it. I wondered then how everyone who lived in the area could just go on with their daily lives when this communication from all the local living things was crying out so loudly. I wondered if anyone else felt this rage and anger."
Stephen Harrod Buhner, Sacred Plant Medicine: The Wisdom in Native American Herbalism

›
THOMAS SCHORR-KON

TRACKING THE FIRST LANGUAGE?

Tracking; the following of foot prints left by people and animals across the surface of the land is possibly one of the oldest pursuits of Earth centred peoples. Following trails in order to know where you are, to find animals for food and to remain safe from enemies are all ways of relating to tracks and tracking. We might consider this to be a primitive skill and assume it is basic and unsophisticated. With this view in mind we may consider any language aspect to only relate to the capacity to identify different species from the shape of a track.

When we study tracking as a practice we discover that we can read far more in a track than we can see if the person or animal is standing in front of us. Not only this we encounter a level of detail and sophistication that we do not encounter in many other areas of life. We find a vocabulary of pressure solidified into shapes that mirror the wave forms of water, tectonic movements in miniature and lines, pocks and domes reminiscent of finger prints. All this information yields different meaning depending on where it appears in the track. This level of detail requires a symbolic means of transmission that could easily have been the first form of alphabet. As tracking is such a primary skill for understanding the comings and goings of the natural world. It is in essence the Earth speaking directly to us of the current events of the day, much like a natural newspaper.

I was running an intensive tracking workshop and we were coming to the end of the first day, when one of the students decided to set a sand trap to catch some animal tracks overnight. That evening we were working on night tracking and I suspect one of our group trod in this sand trap in the course of our night excursion. The student went early to his sand trap only to discover a giant human boot print in the middle of his cleared patch of sand. At first he was a bit disgruntled and then accepted what he had been given and set to examining the track. He had trained in reflexology and as he looked at the big boot print he found some anomalies. He came into breakfast and immediately went round the group checking everyone's boots. Eventually he settled on one of the other students. "do you have a problem with your lungs?" he asked. The fellow student was stunned and went a bit white. "how did you know?" he responded incredulously. "I nearly drowned four years ago and that is why I am on this path now" he went on to share. The student had used his knowledge of reflexology to diagnose the preexisting condition through a thick walking boot. This was before being taught the trackers version of foot mapping. This illustrates the level of conversation that is possible with nature if we take the time to patiently take in the available information.

By insulating ourselves from nature we make it harder to hear her voice. We can live in a trance never really paying attention to anything, or we can start to engage with life, engage with our senses with our world. The conversation with nature is inescapable. If we are having our conversation through replanting forests or driving a bulldozer or sanctioning the destruction of our sources of drinking water by doing nothing to protect them, we are still having it.

In order to have a real communication with nature, a heartfelt conversation, there are a number of issues that if we let go of or move through, allow us to hear the voice of nature. Firstly if we can let go of the notion that everything is dead matter and move to a recognition that nature is infused with the energy that moves in and through all things. We are then faced with a multitude of alive beings to communicate with.

Next, if we can dismantle the hierarchical view of ourselves in relation to nature. The notion that humans have dominion over all things. We are welcomed by the wider community of the natural world as equals. We no longer feel alone, instead there is a feeling of holding and connection. Then there may be our own grief to move through in relation to the current state of the planet. Transforming this by feeling and expressing it, into connection and then possibly action. This opens our heart centre through which our communication with nature can take place. Next we might encounter the grief that the land may hold as we begin our conversation.

A great deal is at stake if we do not manage to regain our capacity to talk and listen to nature, we face grave consequences. Though if we can move into the conversation we come closer to the experience of pure and true nature.

It is curiosity that breeds awareness; it does not kill the cat. It awakens us to finding out about our world. When listening to the natural languages that are spoken and understood by all people living close to the Earth; the languages of atmospheric phenomena, birds, plants and animals we become part of the wider conversation. By paying attention to these aspects they respond, our attention is felt, as we feel when someone is looking at us. In summary a relationship develops and through this relationship a heartfelt connection is formed that invites us deeper. In turn creating an understanding of how to use the language of the heart to communicate with nature. These languages are primary to an awareness of the Earth and help us feel that we are part of the weave of nature.

CHAPTER 3

STALKING ONENESS

My first experience of oneness came from what at first seems like an unlikely source, the practice of stalking. It does not seem like a conventional activity to bring about an experience of oneness but if you consider that the point of stalking is to disappear and merge with the environment then perhaps it is not such a strange outcome to feel yourself crying out to become one with the earth so that you are not perceived as separate from it.

The first time I encountered a need to become one with the earth, was the first time the experience of oneness became powerfully tangible. I had learned and practiced the art of stalking in the Pine Barons of New Jersey. My main worry in that location was encountering an illegal Hunter, sat in his 4x4 with a six pack of beer and a high-powered rifle pointing out the pickups window at me as I moved through the dark. One of the tests we were put through was to stalk through the local dump which is inhabited by wild dogs.

I learned many things during these weeks of training but it wasn't until later that the full significance of the stalking practice became apparent. I was stalking a couple of friends in order to keep my skills at a good level. I had previously warned them that I would stalk into their camp that evening. As I approached within a few feet of them, they were obliviously enjoying themselves round their campfire. I found myself calling out to become one with the earth, to truly be a part of the land, melting my own sense of self into the greater whole, in order to remain beyond sight. I was within a few feet of these friends and removed their axe and melted into the night. I later returned to give back the axe and even then they had not seen or sensed my presence and were somewhat confused as to how it had been removed.

The fear is that in letting go of our sense of self we will lose something.

Yet in letting go of the small self we become the whole. This experience is the gateway to a vast experience of unity.

In the Tao it says; "The scholar gains something every day the man of Tao loses something every day" My understanding here is "let go of something every day".

When we connect and become one with the earth we encounter the potential to feel a connection with the whole of the cosmos.

Unfortunately with the practice of stalking even the word has very bad press. The connotations attached to the terms stalking are very negative. Within the modern urban environment it is classified as an illegal activity. The stalking I refer to is very different to this. Even when we look at stalking in a modern country setting the association with hunting lends it an ominous connotation, because at the end of a successful stalk a beautiful wild animal will be killed. This view is mostly held within urban communities that are very removed from the daily understanding that death feeds life. It is as if our lives are lived largely to avoid any thought of death and stalking is a stark reminder of this and as such it is out of place in modern life and certainly not considered to have any deeper characteristics. The idea that we can be stalked even in the urban context can bring up our feelings of vulnerability and fear.
In the distant past we would have had to rely on a greater awareness, one that found clues in the broader environment, to keep ourselves safe from all manner of predators.

APART OR A PART

There seems to be a great deal of alienation and disconnection in our society today. The cult or culture of the individual is the myth we follow. This gives both a great deal of freedom with infinite choice, yet we have very few working models to follow. We are not bound by tradition by the way things have been done in the past. We are creating the present and future without reference to how we arrived at our current position. We are no longer held by our culture and guided by the wisdom of those who have been through it before. Each family is acting alone to provide everything for themselves, which imposes a huge pressure on family life as there is little wider community and gender support. This is, in part, because things seem to have changed so much. We are no longer connected to place, often living far from our relatives and from where we were born, not connected to any traditions and separated from our ancestors often by historic trauma, like the first and second world wars.

We have even projected our fears of alienation into the realm of fantasy, creating many Alien dramas that force us to unify in the destruction of the aliens. Yet we are the ones who have become the aliens. Do we know or care about the place that we live in ?

Gary Snyder in his essay 'Good, Wild, Sacred', makes the point that the earth is like a tiny oasis in the vastness of space much like the aboriginal watering holes in the outback.

'Like it or not we are all finally '*inhabitory*' on this one small blue-green planet. It's the only one with comfortable temperatures, good air and water, and a wealth of living beings for millions (or quadrillions) of miles. A little waterhole in the Vast space, a nesting place of singing and practice, a place of dreaming. It's on the verge of being totally trashed-there's a slow way and a fast way. It's clearly time to put hegemonial controversies aside, to turn away from economies that demand constant exploitation of both people and resources, and to put Earth first!"

If we do not care for the earth or if we do not know the place that we live in, we are technically lost. When we know where the water we drink comes from, where to look for edible and medicinal plants, how to make all of the things we need from the resources around us, where the good hunting is, then we are not lost. In knowing this in one place we then know what to look for wherever we go on the earth. Your backyard knowledge is transferable.

Alienation comes from a feeling of separation, of feeling apart from what we inhabit. We may feel disconnected from ourselves other people and our environment. In this state of being cut off there is no sense of responsibility for the implications of our actions. So we have a sense of freedom without responsibility. When we enter into an intimate relationship and feel part of, and connected to, another being, there is a sense in which whatever we do to the other we do to ourselves, as the impact of our actions on whatever level directly feeds back to us. If we put out negativity we get it back and if we make the effort to put out positive thoughts and actions then we reap the benefit of these.

What we feel separated from we have no reason to cherish. We may not understand it and then become fearful of it and in doing so want to destroy it. i.e. in our attempt to 'civilise' every other culture and make wilderness into farm land or a tamed garden. It is almost as if the feeling of exclusion causes us to act negatively towards what we are excluded from. We have an attitude of 'who cares'. Like the bad fairy in the fairy stories, who puts a curse on the new born child because she is not invited to the ceremony. This feeling of separation is almost biblical as if we have been ousted from the Garden of Eden by thought alone.

So where does solitude fit into this? If we are not comfortable with ourselves, if we fear being with ourselves then we seek to be included out of fear. Separation is then fraught with pain rather than infused with freedom. We are separated from the main part of the universe that can help us to make a right relationship to the rest of it all; ourselves. In connecting with ourselves we make contact with the place where the real issues lie. When we stand back and look at our situation on Earth from a distance, we may realise how we cannot live without it, that we are all connected through just being here. Then we come to see that we are part of the oneness whether we like it or not.

The only problem is when we *think* we are not part of it all. So the only real separation is in our mind. Yet knowing that might not be enough. We need to be invited to join the party, the celebration. We may even need a way into help us to truly feel a part of it all rather than feeling apart from it all.

"A human being is a part of the whole called by us a 'universe'… A part limited in time and space. He experiences his thoughts and feelings as separated from the rest – a kind of optical delusion of his consciousness. This delusion is a kind of prison for us, restricting us to our personal desires and to affection for a few persons nearest to us. Our task must be to free ourselves from this prison by widening our circle of compassion to embrace all living creatures and the whole of nature in its beauty."

Einstein.

STALKING

Stalking as a practice is very simple. Simple to describe that is, perhaps much more challenging to accomplish than you might think. It is also problematic because the steps are all really simple and we can mistake this simplicity for lack of content but in my experience, if something can be reduced down to real simplicity it is often more profound and closer to principles and the truth. The main principle required is slowing down, slowing right down, slower than you think you need to go. The average stalking step is one minute from start to finish. This is moving very slowly. Moving slowly requires a great deal of poise, balance and strength. The key is to relax the body as much as possible in order to drop the weight down through the body and thus to conserve energy. Having a bodily understanding of good weight distribution and how to walk in a natural way will help our movements to flow, whereas jerky movements will attract attention.

There are a number of components that when put together not only help us to blend with the environment but also bring us into a different state of consciousness that is allied with the natural rhythm of consciousness of nature (including most animals).

WIDE EYED

The gateway to this is in using our eyes in a different way to the normal way we are used to. What is considered the normal way of looking at the world is typically using a very narrow focus of vision. This is largely how predators view the world; eyes front, assessing possible targets, ranges and striking distances. This is not to say we are all in a predatory mind-set. The introduction of more and more viewing screens has only served to reinforce this way of diminishing our potential capacity to use our vision in a more powerful way.

It is our peripheral vision that we need to expand and use more. This is sometimes called wide-angle vision. There are a few groups of people who employ their peripheral vision more than most: battle hardened veterans, martial artists and I suspect some sportsmen and women. It has been scientifically proven that women have much greater peripheral vision than men which puts men at a great disadvantage in respect of shifting into a more intuitive state, which is the state that this shift in the use of the eyes can help to create.

There are a number of things that change when we move into using our peripheral vision not just in our capacity to take in more visual information but it also affects our depth of field, night vision, and state of consciousness, measurably changing our brainwave state.

CONES AND RODS IN THE DARK

Our eyes have two different types of cells, cones and rods and as we move into peripheral vision we start to use the rods more than the cones. These are more sensitive to light therefore we find that our night vision is increased when in peripheral vision.

Because we are not so focused on a particular object or target, our depth of field becomes limitless allowing us to perceive movement beyond the first layer of undergrowth that our eye would normally rest on if we were using our predatory vision. Our attention shifts from paying attention to objects to our attention being drawn by movement. In fact we become hypersensitive to tiny movements which will draw our attention in a way that makes us far more aware of what is going on around us than if we were stuck in our predatory vision. The peripheral vision is more like the vision of most prey animals who are paying a wider attention to the environment because their lives to depend on it. If we look at the skulls of prey animals we find their eyes are set on either side of the skull rather than at the front like predators.

THE NATURAL STEP

If we also put with this another component: a natural way of stepping, sometimes called a 'fox walk' then our consciousness shifts very swiftly into a meditative state. Instead of having to sit in meditation for hours we find that we enter into the alpha state very swiftly. The key to the natural way of stepping is to relax the ankle.

If you stand on one leg lifting your other leg and shake your ankle so that it relaxes and then allow the foot to meet the ground, you will find that it meets the ground in a very different way to the way that you have been used to stepping. What will happen is that the outside edge of the foot will meet the ground first then the foot will roll across from small toe to the large toe as opposed to the heel striking the ground first. This brings with it a great deal of benefit.

The first benefit for the Stalker is that it reduces the amount of sound that is made as the foot hits the ground. Secondly it allows much more control so that if we do begin to make a sound we can stop the sound being made halfway through. We are also employing the full use of all of the bone structures that exist in the foot. If we take all of the bones of the hands and feet and put them together they add up to almost half the bones in the entire body. The bone structures of the feet are designed to absorb a great deal of shock including an entire life time of walking and running. If we walk normally with our feet in coffin-like shoes striking the ground with our heel then we miss the capacity of our body to absorb a vast amount of the shock of each step, causing injury to our bodies over time. Just using these two components of the natural step and peripheral vision (or relaxed vision) change will occur both internally and externally.

NATURE AS MIRROR OR BIO FEEDBACK MECHANISM

The world that we live in is a huge bio feedback mechanism. When our brainwave state is resonant with the natural state, the birds and animals suddenly perceive us as one of them rather than as separate. What are considered normal ways of moving through an urban environment are not understood by the birds and animals. It is felt as threatening therefore they respond in fearful ways making alarm calls, falling silent and flying away screeching. If we enter a natural environment and sit quietly for half an hour, the area will return to its normal baseline and we may well be able to experience signs of things returning to normal: through birds feeding, singing very close to us, perhaps right next to us. This will then signal to the mammals, that it is safe and we might be lucky enough to see a wood mouse run across our foot or have a squirrel drop a nut on us.

As we begin to develop our capacity to stalk the study of the alarm system of nature suddenly opens up to us. So a deep connection starts to form within us as we experience nature undisturbed and up close, perhaps for the first time. This also starts to offer us a repeatable practice or way to be in nature that unlocks her hidden secrets.

We are already able to become more at one with our environment merely by slowing down and acting in a more natural way.

The results of normal human activity cause the birds to fly screeching away from behaviors that they do not understand. This alerts any animals in the vicinity that humans are coming (and we have to remember that we are the number one predator on the planet). If we are hurrying, busy in our minds, we are barely present in the place that we are in. We have brought with us all of the stress and worry from the city into the countryside. This internal disturbance is at odds with the natural rhythm of the earth and stands out like splashing loudly in a quiet pond.

When we are quieter internally and are putting out fewer internal and external signals that create less ripples around us, the natural feedback we get further opens our heart as we witness first-hand a bird singing or feeding its young or some other miraculous natural event.

There are many different stalking steps and what I have described is not really a stalking step it is merely a natural way of moving which should take place at perhaps half the pace that one would normally walk at.

When working with inner city kids I have found that teaching them the rudiments of silent and invisible movement or stalking helps to create an internal shift that makes them more receptive and able to engage. It has a calming and centring effect that makes it possible to work with some of the most difficult to reach students.

WE WANT TO KILL SOMETHING

I remember one particular incident eighteen years ago when I was assisting in a mentoring experiment. Ten boys of mixed ethnic backgrounds who had been excluded from schools in the St Pauls area of London were to be mentored by ten mentors in a beautiful centre in Wales.

Many interesting things occurred over the week from fights breaking out between the boys and the mentors, including when one of the vehicles tires were slashed; to the boys having an egg fight with forty of the fifty eggs that had been bought for the kitchen. One of the boys stole a camera lead and then returned it, a first for him.

TRUE NATURE

As a mentor I had arrived with my own agenda to bring a shamanic element to the work with the boys. I soon realised when I arrived that that made at least ten different agendas and so I decided on the first evening to drop my agenda, I explained my skill-set to the young men and left it to them to initiate any further exploration, letting things take their own course. Much to my surprise by the second night six of the ten boys had invited me into their round house to have a pipe ceremony.

One afternoon two of the boys came up to me and said "We want to go into the woods and kill something!" " Great lets go " I said. This was a great opportunity to teach them some stalking skills. So we found some stout sticks to use as projectiles and went into the woods. We walked for a good twenty minutes without seeing any wildlife. This was no surprise to me I know the difference that a knowledge of stalking makes and how without it the birds will alert any living creature to the presence of an uninitiated human .

After twenty minutes I asked " Have you seen anything?" They replied that they had not. "How stupid of me" I said, " I forgot to show you how to move through the woods without disturbing everything".

I then suggested we try using peripheral vision and fox walking. The boys got it fairly swiftly and we proceeded to move through the forest still not encountering anything. This time we moved more slowly, stopping periodically to listen and scan the woods.

The boys had begun to quieten down, I then realised that I could lead them from the place of "We want to kill something" to a place of connection and meditation. I asked them if they had seen anything to kill yet and they both responded that they had not. So I suggested that if we wanted to see any game that we would need to quieten down our inner noise and if we sat quietly in the forest for a time this would happen. We found a small clearing and commenced to sit while I took them into a relaxing meditative state. We sat for a further half an hour at the end of which both boys were in a deep Alpha state. On the walk back they began to enjoy just being in the woods, noticing various plants and beautiful sights. On the return we came across a sheep in the woods but the blood lust had gone, replaced with a quiet appreciation. We made our way back to the Centre as the sun was setting, one of the boys remarked "Isn't that beautiful" as we gazed at the sunset.

We had moved from the desire to kill to a state of inner peace through the practice of stalking.

It makes me reflect that hunting as it was practiced in the past would have been shared with the young men of the tribe and the need for quieting the mind and moving silently and in tune with the surroundings, would have been very much part of that instruction as well as required in order to eat.

Stalking is slowing down again much more. We are looking to take one step per minute. When I teach stalking to my students, I do not teach them straight away but I allow them some time in the forest in their normal way of being so that when I share with them how to move skilfully in nature they can experience a strong contrast to their state. This helps to overcome the issue of the skills being so simple.

WAVES: A HYPOTHESIS OF CONNECTION

Several things are taking place that are useful to explain more precisely. The first is that the process of slowing down using the key aspects of stalking i.e. wide angle vision and stalking steps, entrains the brain into an Alpha state. The slowing down process also creates greater heart coherence. These are both electromagnetic shifts in the brain and body. These shifts bring the person both into an Alpha brainwave state and help their brainwaves match the natural electromagnetic rhythm of Nature, the ultra-low frequency waves that are resonating in the cavity between the surface of the Earth and the ionosphere.

Understanding how the brainwaves function can help us get a scientific picture of what is going on. Brainwaves have been studied since the 1920's and have been measureable since the invention of the EEG (electric encephalograph) around 70 years ago. Scientists have been using this technology to map brainwave states. So a great deal of research has been done into brainwave states and this has more recently been taken up by the field of neuro science. The best description of brainwaves I have come across is by Ben Fuchs:

"Like all waves, the ones produced by the brain ebb and flow. Electrical bursts "fire" and then cease firing, essentially blinking on and off. The amount of times a burst of brain electricity and its subsequent cessation, turn on and off in every second is called a "cycle" and measured as "cycles-per-second" (CPS). The number of cycles-per-second is referred to as the "frequency". One that fires and stops firing, or cycles once a second, is said to have a frequency of one. If flow and ebb occurs twice a second the frequency would be two….and so on"

Through EEG measurements a spectrum of brainwave states have been measured and identified from 0.5 cycles per second up to 100's of cycles per second. We are going to shine a light just on a small part of the spectrum for the moment to help to understand what is going on when we are stalking.

As well as the brain having electromagnetic pulses or waves, the whole of nature also is resonating in a similar way and it has been suggested by Hainsworth ('The Sedona Effect') that our brainwave patterns have evolved from the electromagnetic resonance of the earth.

Natures electromagnetic resonance was discovered by Winfried Otto Schumannn in 1952 but it was not until 1960/63 that it was finally measured (by Balser and Wagner) and Schumannn's calculations and theories were borne out. The earth's natural resonance was measured to be 7.83 Hz. (Hertz are a measure of the number of cycles per second)

The 'Schumannn Resonance', as it is now known, is caused by the discharge of global lightning strikes, with some 2000 thunderstorms globally discharging around 50 lightning strikes per storm. This electromagnetic energy then resonates between the earth's surface and the ionosphere to create a resonance of 7.83 Hz This has a diurnal fluctuation of about + or - 0.5 Hz. The calculation is arrived at by taking the electromagnetic energy of the lightening (measured at the speed of light) and dividing this by the circumference of the Earth. So for it to fluctuate either the speed of light or the circumference of the Earth needs to substantially change.

If we equate this to the brainwave states then we see they move between the Alpha frequency in the day and the Theta frequency at night. Alpha is between 8-12 Hz. and the Theta frequency is between 4-8 Hz.

So, when our own brainwave frequency is at the Alpha level, we resonate with the natural frequency of the Earth. When the waves in our little pond match the waves that are resonant around us in the larger pond then there is a connection a correlation. Like a radio tuning into a particular station we can receive and be received by others in this resonance.

All of nature is tuned to this resonance and so when we are in an Alpha state nature's feedback systems (the birds and animals) recognise us as part of nature and treat and respond to us as if we are part of and not separate from nature, or a threat.

Nature can also induct us into these brainwave states when we spend time in nature, especially when we are on our own: sitting around the fire, listening to water flow or feeling the wind in our hair. Interestingly, if we are isolated from this rhythm we can suffer serious mental and physical health problems. As was discovered when astronauts first started to travel beyond the ionosphere.

"Studies show that subjects living in isolation from geomagnetic rhythms over long periods of time developed increasing irregularities and chaotic physiological rhythms - which were dramatically restored after the introduction of a very weak 10Hz electrical field. Early astronauts suffered until SR (Schumann Resonance) generators were installed in their space crafts."   Ben Lonetree

By 1974 German scientist Wolgang Ludwig had developed the first Schumannn Resonance product, which was installed in all space crafts by N.A.S.A. The instillation of these generators demonstrates a clear scientific recognition of the importance of the Earth's natural resonance on its inhabitants and their wellbeing.

What Ludwig also found was that while it was easy to measure the Schumann resonance in nature (and on the ocean) it was difficult to measure it in cities. This was because of the increased number of electromagnetic waves generated by humans' electronic devices. Perhaps the Schumann resonance technology could be employed in our inner cities to reduce stress and behavioral problems by reintroducing the natural Earth resonance.

THE HISTORY OF CLOUDS

When we understand that with the diurnal variation of 0.5, the Schumannn resonance is moving between two resonances that relate directly to our own brainwave states. When we are in sleep state we produce a Theta resonance. The range of Theta is from 4 to 8 Hz and Alpha from 8 to 12 Hz.

Hainsworth theorised that it is the Schumannn resonance that has established our brainwave states. When we consider the reverence with which lightning wielding entities have been accorded through history, we find in many cultures a deification of this elemental power. In the Lakota tradition of North America they are known as the Thunder beings, in Norse mythology as Thor and Odin, and in Greek mythology as Zeus; Indra in Hinduism and Shango in the Yoruba religion. This perhaps helps us to understand that the elemental forces, whether we personify them or not, are higher powers that influence our behavior; that we are not acting in the isolated fashion we would like to believe.

ENTRAINMENT

Having watched my students take their first stalking steps many times over the past 20 years, I have noticed that at minute six each time the birds will come near the students and start singing in the trees around them for the first time, after they have already been in the woods for at least twenty four hours.

This left me with the question why six minutes?

My hypothesis so far is that when we slow down to 'stalking speed' and use peripheral vision our brain slows to the Alpha brainwave rhythm. When this rhythm matches the Schumann resonance the birds respond with their normal behaviour as if we were no longer perceived as separate. This is effectively being invisible to the natural alarm system of the forest.

What is left to figure out is why the six minutes that it takes for the birds to respond to the group of students who have merged with the

Schumann resonance?

What we discover is that when we entrain the brain into different states there is a certain time period that this can take.

"Entrainment" is a term from physics which means "the tendency for two vibrating bodies to lock into phase so that they vibrate in harmony". For example, one tuning fork when struck and placed next to another tuning fork will cause the second one to vibrate at the same rate. This was first observed by Dutch scientist, Christian Huygens, in 1665 while he was working on the design of the pendulum clock. He found that when he placed two of the clocks on a wall near each other and swung the pendulums at different rates, they would eventually end up swinging at the same rate.

Brain entrainment is not new, it has been practiced for millennia in a shamanic context and we will go into this in 'The Science of Shamanism'. It has been discovered through modern brain entrainment techniques that when we seek to entrain the brain into a different brainwave state it takes six minutes of entrainment for the brainto shift into a different state.

This is why, by minute six, the students have slowed down into an Alpha state, letting the stalking shift them into the natural brainwave state which is closer to the Schumannn resonance. Then the birds who are one of the most noticeable natural feedback mechanisms of the earth, start to sing, expressing harmony and a zero-threat level from the students.

What this means is that if you slow down for six minutes use peripheral vision and walk naturally or even more slowly you will enter an alpha state with very little effort. This in my opinion is the natural state of consciousness of human beings.

The state that is considered the normal state of human consciousness; a faster speed at which the brain can operate, is called Beta and is 13-30 Hz. (or cycles per second).
For those of us who find it hard to sit still and meditate, who struggle to control our physical minds or to be detached from the thoughts that flow through the mind, the practice of stalking can silence the physical

mind within six minutes or less.

So, we have already learnt that even before we begin to enter stalking speed by acting in natural ways like placing our foot with a relaxed ankle and using our peripheral vision our body and mind respond and start to shift into a slower more natural rhythm. A rhythm that as it turns out is closer to the natural frequency of the Earth.

PREDATOR AND PREY VISION
THE DOORWAY TO INVISIBILITY

The position of our eyes is an indication of the primary way they are intended to be used. Humans are the number one predator on the planet and so our tendency is to use the forward focused vision the position of our eyes predicates. This means we are set up to act and perceive as predators. Most prey animals have their eyes set on either side of their head in order to be able to keep themselves safe. If we compare the skull of a deer, (a prey animal), and the skull of predators such as a fox or cat this becomes very evident. Prey animal's vision is based on detecting movement and less emphasis is placed on finding the exact location of a target. With the position of a prey animals eyes they are in a constantly peripheral, type of vision. When we use peripheral vision we become more sensitive to tiny movements and our depth of field changes from the specific target to infinity. So we can see the similarity between prey vision and our use of peripheral vision.

This is backed up by our own experiences of having the capacity to feel when someone is staring at us (using predatory vision) from behind. As our capacity to sense energy is innate, we all have had experiences of either staring at someone and them turning round to look at us or vice versa.

It is as if, when we use our predatory vision, we are directing the beam of a powerful light, focused on what we are looking at, which can then be felt by the person in the beam. When we look at people and animals with wide angle vision that beam is diffused and it is felt less. The predatory focus is removed and the observed is left more at ease. This becomes the door way to invisibility. This is because our presence is felt less

STALKING

Stalking itself is moving at a much slower pace. We are looking at one minute per step and slower. It always feels to me as if I am growing in a particular direction, rather than stepping. It is when we reach out to non-human states and ways of moving, that we start to blend and merge more with our environment. The less we act like a human the better. The more we mimic the characteristics and movement of animals, or other non-human entities, the less noticeable we are and the more we are read as part of the environment.

The Apache scouts were masters of this art and many of their ways have been passed down. They had a very good understanding of both nature and human psychology which allowed them to pass unnoticed by both man and animals. There is an old Arizonian joke that goes 'How many Apaches are in the room?' The answer is: 'As many as want to be'. Such was their skill, because their lives and the lives of their children depended upon it.

When we consider the genuine stalking step we need to break the step down into more stages. The placing of the foot is divided into four parts: the outside edge, inside edge, heel then lastly the toes. Once these four stages of foot placement have happened the weight is shifted onto the foot. If you imagine walking in extreme slow motion this is closer to the sort of experience that stalking is. Yet it is not just walking, it also involves crawling and belly crawling and moving at different heights and levels depending on the cover that the environment affords us or what we are stalking.

When we are immersed in the Alpha state there is a level of absorption that can be achieved which negates many physical barriers and allows us to overcome even extreme physical conditions. I remember one class when I was teaching stalking, a huge thunderstorm passed by releasing the weight of water carried by the clouds. We were scheduled to go on an overnight stalking mission. I remember the students looking at me as if to say "You're not going to send this out in that", and of course we went out to accomplish the exercise anyway.
What I remember on the return, once everyone was back safely and I was back in Camp. Was that it was only then I realised I was completely soaked through to the skin. At the point that I came out of the Alpha state, the physical conditions suddenly became apparent and

I felt the cold soaked through sensation of my clothes.
There are also specific training methods which utilise this state to develop skills i.e. walking blindfold over a balance beam.

What I have found is that speech impairs the Alpha state. It tends to bring us out of the state of absorption and back into a Beta state. The Apache scouts were well aware of this and used different forms of communication that did not involve speaking. When these types of communication are used, the brain remains in an Alpha state.

If we move continuously in a straight line through the undergrowth then it is very easy to perceive our movement and our destination. If, on the other hand, we flow with the foliage being moved by the landscape and take time to survey and enjoy the areas that we are passing through the majesty of the night, the beauty of a plant or track then our journey is broken up and our presence is scattered across the landscape rendering our destination unclear to any observer. If we move in this way following our natural curiosity and excitement at what is going on in the landscape we find that we learn more as we move through the landscape and we are less obtrusive.

Thus we have changed the way we use our body by slowing it down and relaxing our movement. By using our eyes differently we also affect the resonance of our mind, again relaxing and slowing down the speed at which it operates.

SURRENDER TO

The practice of stalking has many physical components and training methods yet, the most powerful element that all of these skills direct us towards, is the ability to surrender. The whole concept of surrender usually brings up huge amounts of resistance. Again it is a big concept and difficult to get a handle on. One of the main methods used to practice surrender and develop our inner guidance is the blind fold.

I was training a group in stalking and nature awareness skills; they were blind folded and placed in dense areas of trees and undergrowth about 400 yards from where I sat, slowly beating a drum. They all stalked in blind folded, bare foot with the minimum of clothing on, just shorts and a tee-shirt. One woman arrived at the drum and I whispered that she could remove her blindfold. This she did and put on her glasses. The next step she took she stepped on a thorn! She had just walked unscathed over the same thorny ground, through brambles, blindfolded and the moment her sight returned she stopped surrendering. She shifted out of the state of connection and back into opposition.

I was undergoing a similar exercise as part of my training though this time we were stalking through a swamp. At one point in the exercise I felt to remove my blindfold. As far as I was concerned I was on solid ground and out of curiosity wanted to see where I was. Imagine my surprise when I discovered that I was negotiating my way from the bank across a small river and had found the only solid ground, a partially submerged log, reaching across the middle of the stream. I was not even aware that I had the stream in front of me to cross and that my next step would have been in the water.

The problem we are faced with, if we do not have a physical practice to help us to develop our ability to surrender, is what do we surrender to? Like with blind faith, we do not want to just believe without any basis for our belief. Yet here we have discovered that blindfolding gets us into the state necessary to surrender. Here is the key: we are *surrendering to* something in particular. We are surrendering to the Earth. It is a small step (a stalking step) from here to surrender to Love or surrender to peace, oneness or awakening.

The important factor is that we are *surrendering to* something. This removes the nebulous quality of surrender that usually makes us back off from it altogether.

TRUE NATURE

ONENESS WITH A BLADE OF GRASS

A CONVERSATION

"How do we move towards an experience of oneness?"

For me the most tangible experiences of oneness have come from the practice of stalking. The concept of oneness appears so big that it seems impossible to start our journey towards it, yet we are a part of the unity of all things and it is usually only our mind that tries to persuade us (through the thought patterns we choose to believe) that we are separate. Not believing our thoughts is a crucial part of this process, both in the moment and in unpicking various thought forms which we have internalised and operate from.

Not believing our unsolicited thoughts is a practice that takes time to develop. The use of peripheral vision quietens the mind and reduces the amount of thoughts moving through the mind. When we start to disbelieve thoughts that direct us towards worry and negative thinking or even anticipation of positive outcomes we are instead directed back into the present. Worrying is effectively praying for things we don't want.

The belief that we are part of a hierarchy with Heaven above us and the animals underneath and with plant life beneath that, reinforces our sense of separation. Being 'above' the animals, plants, rocks and trees makes it difficult for us to relate to them. Yet our dependence on these elements and beings, means that we cannot do without them. If we are introduced to them, getting to know their beauty, skill and power, we can start to appreciate them. From this grows a respect and even a kinship. We start to recognise that we share this place with many other benevolent beings. We can let go of some of our hierarchical notions and embrace a concept, based on a view of equality. Yet this is quite difficult for the western mind to accept.

"You mean we are the same as a blade of grass?"

Any fool can see the difference between a human and a blade of grass, yet it takes a great leap to be able to see the interconnectedness of all things and to be able to experience the act of life giving to itself as it does when we eat anything, even a blade of grass. What creates the equality is unseen, (and it is culturally unseen), that matter is infused with spirit. We can be trapped in a world where all we perceive around us is dead matter or we can exist in a world of energy and spirit and live a full spectrum life. Again this is a matter of what we think, which determines how we interpret our experiences writing off synchronicities as coincidence or fluke, rather than exploring their potential.

> "What do you mean a blade of grass has a spirit??!"

We are not talking about the mind/body split here put forward by Socrates (who was condemned to death by the first democracy in Greece for asking dangerous questions) it is the spirit/mind/body split we are seeking to address. Now mind here comes between body and spirit as it often can. We could even go so far as to suggest that there is a Spirit/energy/mind/body split that needs addressing between all components of full spectrum living.

> "You mean a blade of grass has all this?"

Well there has been a considerable amount of research to show that plants feel pain. They also respond to love, being caressed and talked to. For me, the route to feeling and understanding the unity of all things through my connection with the plants, has for the most part been in developing an understanding of their healing virtues. As I discovered and used the so called 'weeds' that grow everywhere as powerful medicines, often using one plant to treat a wide variety of ailments, I realised that what they provide we cannot do without. i.e. a tree stands for hundreds of years enriching the environment, creating the very air we breathe. When we look beneath the surface, even just on a physical level, we encounter such a depth of resources that I now find it hard to eat, as food, some of the wild edible plants because of the respect I have for their healing powers.

> "You mean a blade of grass is a healer now? Do eat grass, don't eat grass, let's call the whole thing off!"

All we are seeking is a sense of equality. To feel, not that we are the same as a blade of grass, but to feel the *life-force* of a blade of grass. To acknowledge that our life-force and the life-force of a blade of grass have the same source. To cast aside the view that we are superior to what we depend on, perhaps we can then be open to experiencing this unity.

Tom Brown JR in his introduction to his guide to edible and medicinal plants relates the moving story of his first hunt and the killing of a young deer. He has selected and got to know intimately not only its patterns of movement (that lead to its death), but he has become so much a part of the background that it accepts and trusts him. When he finally kills the deer with a spear, at close range he is totally repulsed by his actions. On returning to his mentor, Grandfather…..

"As I walked up the path to camp, I caught sight of Grandfather leaning against a tree, watching me. In a way I hated him for making me kill in this way. As I drew closer, I made no attempt to hide my tears but gazed right into his eyes. For a fleeting moment, I caught the same glimmer the deer had in his eyes, the all-knowing feeling. He plainly saw my pain and suffering. He sensed myriads of questions flowing through my mind, as I know now he must have had at one time. He pointed an old and gnarled finger at me and said "Grandson, when you can feel the same pain and suffering for a blade of grass ripped from the Earth as you do for that deer, you will truly be one with all things."

> "We need to kill a blade of grass now, to become one with it??"

In order to live we need to kill things. It is not that we need to stop this, as death feeds life, it is the way in which we take life that is crucial.

If we take it with care and reverence then we are honouring the parts of nature we are taking. Then eating and sharing food becomes a communion.

"To live, we must daily break the body and shed the blood of Creation. When we do this knowingly, lovingly, skillfully, reverently, it is a sacrament. When we do it ignorantly, greedily, clumsily, destructively, it is a desecration. In such desecration we condemn ourselves to spiritual and moral loneliness, and others to want."
Wendell Berry, *The Art of the Commonplace: The Agrarian Essays*

ALPHA BREATH DYNAMICS

In the last year I have come to develop an intervention called Alpha Breath Dynamics. It has grown out of my understanding of Stalking, Meditation and Martial Arts.

Through studying what occurs while stalking and isolating the components it is possible to enter an Alpha state fairly rapidly with no external intervention i.e. without brainwave entrainment etc.

Having meditated for many years and found how powerfully calming the effects of slowed breathing could be I started to experiment with the stalking movements broken down into segments timed with the breath. While stalking the breath naturally slows so it seemed to be a natural point of focus. I began working with a in breath of between 4-5 seconds and an out breath of the same length. I found my state shift seemed to be sped up by this approach within two steps i.e. in after two minutes I felt the effects of the Alpha state.

However trying to coordinate the stalking movements with the breath was quite complicated and moving in slow motion, especially standing on one leg has its challenges. I wanted to simplify the process cut away anything unnecessary. So I retained the peripheral vision element from stalking but let go of the attempt at stepping.

Instead I began to experiment with different movements taking simple Chi Gung exercise like raising and lowering the hands in coordination with the breath. It was at this point that I realised I was entering an Alpha state within ten to twelve breaths. This is under two minutes. While the normal entrainment time through stalking or external methods is about six minutes.

The first test that I ran with this new information was at an event in London. I have a brainwave measuring machine called a 'mind ball'. By put on a head band with sensors in it and shifting into an Alpha state a ball moves along a triangular base to stop in an end zone.

The event was Buddhist based and so I thought there would be experienced meditators present. People tried with mixed success. Towards the end of the day two teenagers came over. They had been watching for some time and wanted to have a go. I let them try and watched them have no success for about ten minutes, I then suggested they try using peripheral vision, slowing their breath and synchronising their hand movements to the breath. Within two minutes they were having success moving the ball.

This gave me food for thought: had I found a swift way to help anyone enter the Alpha state and who would this most benefit?

The second test I ran was at another event later the same year. I got talking to young men one who had both A.D.H.D. and Asperger's.

I offered to show him my simple intervention and after some reassurance he agreed. After a few minutes of practice he was dramatically changed. He said he had never felt so calm in his life.

It was a few minutes after this that he broke down revealing to me and his friend that he had been sexually abused as a child and had shared this information with very few people.

I had previously theorized that A.D.H.D. seemed to mean that the young person was locked into a Theta state and a few years after developing this theory, had found evidence that this was the case and that brainwave entrainment was being used to help people with this condition develop access to Alpha. When I came across the information explained on page 119 about brainwaves and age I developed the hypothesis that if a child is traumtised between the ages of 4 -8 they will stay in the Theta state as it provides resources and sensitivities that the child does not want to let go of. Hence the trauma resurfacing once an Alpha state is achieved.

This brings into focus the need for professional support for those trying out these techniques if trauma is the cause.

CHAPTER 4

THE SCIENCE OF SHAMANISM

"Wildness we might consider as the root of the authentic spontaneities of any being. It is that wellspring of creativity whence comes the instinctive activities that enable all living beings to obtain their food, to find shelter, to bring forth their young: to sing and dance and fly through the air and swim through the depths of the sea. This is the same inner tendency that evokes the insight of the poet, the skill of the artist and the power of the shaman."

Thomas Berry

BEYOND BELIEF

A shaman is someone who has transcended the path they have chosen to follow to arrive at their knowledge and power. This means that any spiritual path can lead to this destination.
The shaman's goal is self-mastery, the true knowledge of the self. This goal leads to an inquiry into the full spectrum of being human. It starts a quest to explore all the inner and outer worlds that we inhabit, in order to fuse with these multiple levels. Nature is both guide and proving ground in this quest, as it provides the wider context and the first level of oneness through stalking. Like a mirror, the natural world reflects us back to ourselves and in its untamed, unconditioned, aspect ultimately points to our true nature.

"I believe that the greater part of man's existence is in the spirit realm, the worlds of the unseen and eternal. It is the larger and purer part of life that makes life full and whole and makes man "one" with all things.... Man has lost his connection to that world and thus his communication and power. This world of spirit cannot be understood through the words and concepts of man, nor can it be understood by logical thought. It can only be entered through the heart and pure mind." Tom Brown JR

When we encounter stories that resonate with us, they can be a useful guidepost. If we are overly sceptical of them or too eager to believe what we read, we miss the point. The story might bring us closer to the possibility of the experience. I heard a story about an Aboriginal tracker who was asked to track an expedition in the outback that had taken place years before. He dutifully followed the trail explaining where camps had been made etc much to the amazement of one of the anthropologists who had been on the original expedition. He was asked how he did it, and replied "I just went back in time and followed you folks". As if it was the most natural thing in the world. I enjoyed the story and would have loved to know how that was possible. At a certain point in my training I was shown techniques for going back in time. Sometime later I was about to run a nature connection class and arrived at the barn where all my equipment was stored, to find there was a different combination lock on the door, now with an extra digit. I thought that as a scout if I could not get into the barn to get my kit I did not deserve to run the class. So I shifted back in time to see the combination the last person had used to undo the lock and I had the lock open within a few minutes.

I am only relaying the story here to illustrate that we can enjoy or resonate with a story, and then perhaps at another time, we hear a similar story from someone we meet, bringing the experience a bit closer. Only when we seek to learn how to re-enact or practice what we have heard as a story, do we discover if it has any truth or reality to it. Then if we find we can duplicate the experience in some way, we have brought it to life. Put another way: I encourage you not to believe any of the stories you read; run your own experiments, and if required get some instruction. Then you are going beyond belief and developing your own knowledge. Then your belief rests on your experience and becomes an unshakable faith. Shamanic practice relies on this process, belief is not required, just the capacity to still the mind enough to experience states that are considered to be no-ordinary reality.

DREAMS, IMAGINATION AND THETA

Before I began to study with one of my most influential teachers Tom brown JR I went to New York with my friend Poppy. My father had died and I had some of his affairs to sort out there. During this trip I encountered an experience that I could not explain away. It was both lucid and extremely useful.

We were staying in the Algonquin hotel in a tiny room with twin beds with just enough room to stand up between them. The first night we were there I dreamt that I walked down the corridor and entered another room. This room was like an apartment with a sitting room and a little kitchen area and a separate bedroom at the back. I woke in the morning and said to my friend Poppy, "Do you suppose they have self-catering apartments to rent in this hotel?" he replied that this was New York and that they had everything here. So after breakfast we went to the main desk and asked if they had self-catering apartments to rent, they said that they did, at this point I wanted to test out my dream and see if the room I had walked into in the dream was the same in reality. So I enquired if they had one of these suites on our floor. They said yes and that it was empty and so we proceeded to take a look. My excitement grew as we came to the door, the one that I had gone through in my 'Dream'. This was the door to the self-catering unit on our floor. So at least I had got that part right. As we entered I was astonished to discover that the room was laid out exactly as I had seen it in the 'dream'. We came into the sitting room, with the kitchen to the left and extra bed room at the back. We decided to move to this room and when we were installed I told my friend Poppy about my experience the night before.

It was some time before I could understand what had happened and not until I began my training with Tom Brown JR that I was able to duplicate the experience consciously. This being one of the first things we learned on the path of the shaman.

Experiences of this kind are innate and most people have had some kind of experience akin to this. The type of experience I refer to here is when we have access to information that we could not gain physically. These unexplained experiences we tend to write of as coincidence or synchronicity at best. Yet they are sign posts to the possibilities that are available to us with in the sphere of spirit.

When we dream we are not bound by the normal physical limitations we encounter in our waking life. Neither are we subject to the constraints of linear time. We can dream we are flying, breathing underwater, visiting relatives from the past or being shown precognitive experiences from the future. On waking we largely find that it is through decoding the symbols of our dreams that we can find meaning that applies to our lives. The dreams may also carry feelings, expressing anxieties we haven't admitted to ourselves or good feelings that affirm choices we were faltering to make. Sometimes our dreams are far more direct in their communication creating synchronicities that we struggle to explain away.

When we are in REM sleep (rapid eye movement) the 'dreaming state', where we have most of our vivid dreams our brainwave state will be equivalent to Theta. Scientists consider that this state gives us access to our unconscious and its potential. The Theta state is associated with: deep relaxation, out of body experiences, spiritual connection and insight. It is also possible through hypnosis to reduce the pain threshold in Theta through (Hypnoanasthesia) to be able to carry out surgery without the patient feeling pain. It is also possible to achieve levels of healing that are currently beyond the understanding of allopathic scientific medical practice.

It is also strongly connected to the power of the imagination hence increasing creativity. Our capacity to learn new things or change behaviors in this state may only need one repetition in order to be assimilated whereas in a normal state we may need many repetitions.

When we examine the processes by which some of the greatest scientists have come up with their different perspectives. Perspectives, that in the process of their discovery, move beyond carefully concealed assumptions implicit in their predecessors viewpoints and often challenge the status quo. We discover that the imagination and/or dreaming plays a vital role in moving beyond previous conceptions. If we take the exponential shift from Newtonian physics to Einstein's discoveries, which have subsequently open the door for quantum physics, we find that Einstein's process of discovering new ground, though scientifically rigorous, were rooted in the imagination. He practised thought experiments in an imaginative dreamlike state where visualisation and feeling were primary. Only later translating this into language in order to explain the thought experiments and later working out a mathematical framework for those ideas.

Einstein is famous for saying,
"Imagination is more important than knowledge". And
"We cannot solve our problems with the same thinking we used when we create them",

When we look more closely at his own descriptions of his thought processes it becomes clear that his discoveries are rooted in his use of his imagination, as if they are plucked from the Theta state and then described and given a mathematical basis or proof.

"The words all the language, as they are written or spoken, do not seem to play any role in my mechanism of thought. This psychical entities which seemed to serve as elements and thought are certain signs and more or less clear images which can be 'voluntarily' reproduced and combined."

"The above-mentioned elements are, in my case, visual and some of muscular type. Conventional words or other signs have to be sought for laboriously only in the secondary stage, when the mentioned associative play is sufficiently established and can be reproduced at will... (My typical thinking style is) visual and motoric. In a stage when words intervene at all, they are, in my case, purely auditive, but they interfere only in a secondary stage as already mentioned."

Albert Einstein "letters to Jacques Hadamard" the creative process edited by Brewster Ghiselin, Mentor books, New American library, New York, New York 1952 P 43 strategies of genius volume 2 Robert B Dilts page 49

He goes on to explain that this playful imaginative way of developing ideas, does not necessarily mean they are true, the verification of the thought experiments comes afterwards and that there is a transition from dreaming to thinking that is characterised by the use of words. Einstein considers this a step down, in order to be able to communicate the ideas which are largely being developed visually and through feeling.

"... All our thinking is of this nature of free play with concepts; the justification for this play lies in the measure of survey over the experience of the senses which we are able to achieve with its aid. The concept of truth cannot yet be applied to such a structure"

Albert Einstein, autobiographical notes Albert Einstein philosopher - scientist by Paul Arthur Schilpp, North western University press Evanston, III 1949 page 7

"I think that the transition from free association or 'dreaming' to thinking is characterised by the more or less dominating role which the 'concept' plays in it. It is by no means necessary that a concept must be connected with a sensorial and cognizable reproductive sign (i.e. Word); but when this is the case thinking becomes by means of that fact communicable.

Albert Einstein strategies of genius volume 2 Robert B Dilts page 57

So surprisingly we are uncovering a way of working that is akin to visualisation with a strong feeling sense. This is largely the approach used to enter a Theta state. As if a waking dream was being entered consciously, in order to try to understand the mysterious workings of the world. My point here is to illustrate, using one of the most preeminent scientists of our age, how the source of his genius and major discoveries can be attributed to a skilful use of his imagination. With the scientific rigour and mathematical proof being applied after the fact, to support the new discovery. This throws into question the overtraining of our physical and logical minds and the diminished position that imagination seems to play both in education and in its potential being recognised as something of value in our society. When we begin to harness the power of our imagination a great deal more becomes possible.

"Logic will get you from A to B, imagination will take you everywhere else"
Einstein

If we also include here the work of Tesla a scientist who uncovered and developed a vast array of scientific advances that we now take for granted. He was overshadowed by more unscrupulous businessmen such as Edison. Tesla worked for Edison in his career and superseded Edison's development of DC current with his own development of AC current, which was able to be sent over much longer distances, without loss of voltage. Similarly the discovery of the radio was attributed to Marconi, though Tesla had already lodged patents covering the work that Marconi later claimed was his own.

"Tesla was a pioneer in many fields. The Tesla coil, which he invented in 1891, is widely used today in radio and television sets and other electronic equipment. ... His alternating current induction motor is considered one of the ten greatest discoveries of all time. Among his discoveries are the fluorescent light, laser beam, wireless communications, wireless transmission of electrical energy, remote control, robotics, Tesla's turbines and vertical take-off aircraft. Tesla is the father of the radio and the modern electrical transmissions systems. He registered over 700 patents worldwide. His vision included exploration of solar energy and the power of the sea. He foresaw interplanetary communications and satellites."

Dr. Ljubo Vujovic Nikola Tesla 'The genius who lit the world'

What was remarkable about Tesla's approach was his ability to run experiments in his imagination, forgoing the need to build many prototypes, as he would make adjustments in his mind in order to get the results that we now rely upon. It was also his practice not to write down many of his discoveries and to retain the plans in his memory.

"Tesla was gifted with intense powers of visualization and exceptional memory from early youth on. He was able to fully construct, develop and perfect his inventions completely in his mind before committing them to paper. "

Dr. Ljubo Vujovic Nikola Tesla 'The genius who lit the world'

There are other ways in which imagination has been used to achieve great things, in the realm of sports we find many such examples. The one I've chosen here comes from Mike Tyson's autobiography in which he makes it clear that the interesting and unusual training methods of Cus Damato, his trainer, were reliant on the power of his imagination.

Cus Damato used visualisation, hypnosis and affirmations to build Mike Tyson's inner resources. Tyson refers to this as developing his spiritual Warrior. Cus and Tyson worked with the hypnotist John Halpin and Cus used an approach that involved Tyson leaving his body in a visualisation and viewing the fight from above in order to determine the outcome of the fight. In this extract Cus describes his first fight and how he came to understand the method that he then used to train Mike Tyson.

"He got into the ring and his heart was beating like a drum, the bell rang and the other guy charged him and he got knocked around. His nose was swollen, his eye was shut, He was bleeding. The guy asked him if he wanted to go a second round and Cus said he'd try. He went out there and suddenly his mind became detached from his body he was watching himself from afar. The punches that hit him felt like they were coming from a distance. He was more aware of them than feeling them.
Cus told me that to be a great fighter you had to get out of your head. He would have me sit down and he'd say, "Transcend. Focus. Relax until you see yourself looking at yourself. Tell me when you get there".

That was very important for me I'm way too emotional in general later on I realised that if I didn't separate from my feelings inside the ring I would be sunk I might hit a guy with a hard punch and then get scared if he didn't go down.

Cus took this out of body experience one step further. He would separate his mind from his body and then visualise the future." Everything gets calm and I'm outside watching myself" He told me." It's me, but it's not me, as if my mind and body aren't connected, but they are connected. I get a picture in my mind, what it's going to be. I can actually see the picture, like a screen…"

I can take a fighter who is just beginning and I can see exactly how he'll respond. When that happens, I can watch a guy fight and I know everything there is to know about this guy, I can actually see the wheels in his head. It's as if I'm that guy, I'm inside him."
He even claimed that he could control events using his mind. Cus

trained Rocky Graziano when he was an amateur. One time, Cus was in Rocky's corner and Rocky was taking a beating. After being knocked down twice, Rocky came back to the corner and wanted to quit. But Cus pushed him out for the next round, and before Rocky could quit, Cus used his mind to will Rocky's arm to throw a punch and it connected and the guy went down and the reff stopped the fight. This was the heavy dude who was training me."
P47 Undisputed truth

This description of being able to allow an aspect of the self to exit the body and view it from outside is undoubtedly a powerful use of the imagination. The term visualisation is perhaps not strong enough, envisioning is the word I prefer to use for this type of activity. To then be able to view the future outcome, of in this case, the fight and move physical events towards this is a powerful use of imagination.

The predominant brainwave state associated with this transcendence and extreme visualisation is the Theta state. Within the shamanic perspective there is no physical limitation in this state and no time. Tyson is demonstrating the development of the capacity to move beyond physical limitation and to visualise the future in order to manifest it. Whether we believe the envisioning and development of his capacity as a spiritual Warrior, helped him to achieve his heavyweight title of the world is another matter. Though there are similar activities with much documented evidence that support the view that this type of envisioning is possible and workable even for the those sceptical of the process.

If a person imagines themselves to be in a specific location far away from their actual location and then begins to describe details of what they see. The use of the imagination to collect information that is effectively viewed remotely, perceiving details or events that are taking place elsewhere is known as remote viewing.

The Pentagon funded several scientists to run a remote viewing program from 1978 to 1995 and amassed a huge amount of data over the twenty three years the program ran. The Pentagon developed this program in order to be able to spy on the Russians during the Cold War, as they believed the Russians were also working on this type of espionage.

"The SR I remote viewing program ... Carried on for twenty three years, behind a wall of secrecy that is still erected. It had been funded entirely by the government, first under Puthoff, then Targ and finally Edwin May, a burly nuclear physicist who carried out other intelligence work before. In 1978, the army had its own psychic spying intelligence unit in place, code-named grill flame, possibly the most secret program in the Pentagon,"

The Field Lynne McTaggart P 214

The astonishing conclusion of this twenty three years' of research was that anyone could accomplish this with a little bit of training and a relaxed atmosphere. Swann an accomplished psychic worked on remote viewing experiments that went as far as viewing Jupiter before the NASA probe arrived there and Swann reported seeing the ring around Jupiter that the NASA probe discovered when it arrived.

"Human beings, talented or otherwise, appeared to have a latent ability to see anywhere across any distance. The most talented remote viewers clearly could enter some framework of consciousness, allowing them to observe scenes anywhere in the world. But The inescapable conclusion of their experiments was that anyone had the ability to do this, if they were just primed for it – even those highly sceptical of the entire notion. The most important ingredient appeared to be a relaxed, even playful atmosphere which deliberately avoided causing anxiety or nervous anticipation in the viewer. And that was all, other than a little practice. Swann himself had learned over time how to separate signal from noise – somehow divining what was his imagination from what was clearly in the scene (that he was remote viewing)."

The Field Lynne McTaggart P 204

Interestingly, the scientists discovered the importance of the playful atmosphere somewhat like a game, rather than a serious adult pursuit. This is rather reminiscent of children's capacity to imagine. This quality of imagining is also very similar to what occurs when we dream. The link between imagining and dreaming is united by the Theta brainwave state. Visualisation with feeling or envisioning when done correctly induces the Theta state. I have found in my teaching of these skills that the playful approach exponentially increases the results of students. The problem my students encounter more than anything is the capacity to differentiate between the verifiable information they receive and what they are adding in. As Swann refers to in the above quote, he developed the capacity to separate signal from noise, this is what takes time, a kind of calibration process. Lynn Mc Taggart in her book the Field goes on to makes the link between dreams and the use of this type of envisioning.

"Because the information is received by our unconscious mind, we often receive it as we would in a dream state, a memory or a sudden insight – a flash of an image portion of the whole."

The Field Lynne McTaggart P 210

The key to developing the capacity to differentiate between clear information or signal and the background noise of our physical mind is to accept what we receive without grasping. If we are trying to hard we will invariably add information that is irrelevant. If we are surprised by the information this is usually a good sign that it is not something we have made up.

The worst thing a remote viewer could do was to interpret or analyse what they saw. This tended to colour his impressions as the information was still filtering through, and invariably he would guess wrong.

The Field Lynne McTaggart P 208

In my shamanic training I was taught that there were three main distortions that would occur when the physical mind was not quiet enough and sought to jump in and interpret the results of remote viewing, in an attempt to be helpful. This always resulted in a muddying of the waters and there were three specific ways in which this occurred.

The first is mirror imaging, where the target that is remotely viewed appears the opposite way round. Interestingly, the scientists working on the remote viewing project also found this to be a common error.

"The information in their experiments was received in bits and often imperfectly. Although the basic information came through, sometimes the details were a little blurred. Usually the scene was flipped so that the subject would see the reverse, as though looking at the scene through a mirror."

The Field Lynne McTaggart P 208

The second distortion that we were told could occur, was that we might view something at a different time than the present. For example we might enter a house where alterations had taken place and view it prior to those alterations. This was called a time lock, where our focus point or lock shifted from our intention to a different time. Hal Puthoff and Russell Targ also discovered a number of remote viewing experiments in which the viewers reported scenes of architectural structures that had existed at the sites in the past, but that no evidence of them remained on the current site.

"When Pat 'saw' the site, he saw it as it had been 50 years ago, even though all evidence of the water purification plant had long since disappeared."
The Field Lynne McTaggart P 214

What this indicates and a number of studies demonstrate, is that not only is it possible for people to be able to see what is going on over vast distances, but also that they can accurately perceive things that have taken place in the past and perceive things that have yet to happen. As previously stated in the Theta state the shamanic view is that there is no time or physical limitation. From a shamanic perspective this state is called Spirit.

"The same had occurred with PEAR's and SRI's remote viewing studies. Remote viewers were able to see across countries, over continents – even out into space.
But the Pat Price study was an example of something even more extraordinary. The research that was emerging from labs such as PEAR and SR I suggested that people could 'see' into the future or reach back into the past."
The Field Lynne McTaggart P 214

The third distortion I have not found mentioned in the research and this is what we call a depth perception conflict. This occurs when either the remote viewer sees a small detail as something immense or a major feature of the landscape as something small.
The best illustration of this I have encountered is a story of two shepherds who are resting by a stream when one of them falls asleep, in his dream he travels down to the edge of a vast sea through an immense forest, then seeing a series of islands, travels from one to the next until eventually he finds himself in a magnificent white palace.

When he wakes from his dream he tells the other Shepherd what he has dreamt.

The second Shepherd who remained awake, says that to him it looked as if a small butterfly have flown out of the other Shepherd's mouth and had flown down through the long grass to the edge of the stream that they were resting beside and had hopped from one stepping stone to the next, until it had entered a sheep's skull that lay on the other side of the stream, it had then returned just before the other Shepherd woke up.

BRAINWAVES AND AGE

From when we are born our brainwave states change as we grow and develop. There is various information available on this, yet I suspect that these developmental stages are different for each individual and the accounts I have found vary considerably. So what I provide here is a general framework that helps us look at this development.

From birth to the age of 2-4 years old children are predominantly in the delta state. The Delta brainwave speed is from 0.5-4 Hz. Interestingly in this state growth hormone production is triggered. The childs brain is 95% grown by the age of four. It is the slowest brainwave state and closest to the deepest states of consciousness. We could say it is the unconditioned state.

Children then start to shift into Theta from the point when they develop the capacity for speech. Though it is the development of imagination that demarks the transition into Theta as the dominant brainwave state. From this point until 7-8 years old they are largely in the Theta state. We can observe the insatiable capacity children have during this age range for imaginary games, stories and play.

Between the ages of 8-12 they shift predominantly into the Alpha state which is characterised by a concentrated focus and adsorption. So the capacity for connection with focus and flow develop.

Beyond 12-14 they start to engage with the Beta brainwave state, this really develops at the onset of puberty. Signaling a move to self-consciousness. This is considered the normal state of consciousness by western culture.

It is clear that our involvement with the Theta state is a natural part of our development and is unfortunately discouraged as we grow up and become educated. What this also demonstrates is the connection between imagination and the Theta state. It is as if the imagination is the gateway to the Theta state, this childlike state which I would characterise as a state of wonder.

I find that when I am working with students to develop their capacity to move into and resonate with the Theta state the more they can put aside their physical mind and approach each exercise like a game as if they were a child the more successful they are in their attempts.

From the Shamans perspective the Theta resonance is akin to the Spirit realm. As we run various exercises or experiments and find we are capable of remote viewing or other practices, our belief both in our capacity to connect and our ability to work with Spirit increase. We are building our belief, not taking anything on trust. When we can lighten our attitude to one of wonder and acceptance our journey into spirit becomes easy. If we are trying to drag with us the sceptical logical operations of our physical mind, we find that they act like chocks keeping us from taking off into the air space of Spirit. As we become more proficient we can learn to embody this state physically, in order to overcome physical limitations and time, moving and acting in Spirit.

There are also downsides to the Theta state, the daydreaming quality that it holds can lead to an unfocused lack of presence in the moment, and also the slower brainwave pattern is sometimes associated with depression. Young people with ADD and ADHD have been found to exhibit a dominance of Theta brainwave states. Retraining them to be able to change their state into Alpha has shown good results. The excessive energy of attention deficit hyperactivity disorder is also a characteristic of the Theta state. When we use this consciously we can access far more energy than normal and find we don't need to recharge. People with ADHD also exhibit a lack of focus, but with this comes a great deal of sensitivity both to other people's moods, to the sudden appearance of a hawk in the sky, or to uncovering the hiding place of an instructor in the Woods. When we are stuck in the Theta brainwave state and are not experiencing the other parts of the spectrum it seems to become a problem. I hypothesise that this is caused by trauma having been experienced during the period of development when the child is between the age of 4 to 8 when they are predominantly in a Theta state. This trauma then somehow affects the child's ability to develop the Alpha brainwave pattern. The Theta brainwave state may feel safer with its imaginary context, access to a great deal of energy and with the capacity to feel less pain. Theta also gives us deep access to our intuition making it possible for us to receive information that there is no way we could consciously know. Thus providing information to the child that can keep them safe, in situations that have the potential to be traumatic.

SHAMANISM AND THE THETA STATE

From a shamanic perspective we have the capacity in a Theta state to re-imagine our world and seek other perspectives that are not available from our normal vantage point of consciousness. If we take the characteristics of the dreaming state, of no time and no physical limitation, and find a methodology whereby we can reorganise our view of things and then empowered that view, we find that things in the physical world are altered by this process.
This means that we have a choice; either we can awaken in a dreaming state and work from inside this vivid inner world to affect reality, or we can develop a process of engaging the imagination in a way that creates a vividness that goes beyond visualisation, that can affect change at a physical level.

The distinction between these two approaches are known in the shamanic world as the difference between the school of dreaming and stalking.

These are two of the three schools of shamanism, the third is the use of 'teaching plants'. Plants like ayahuasca, san pedro, psilocybin and peote.
These plants bring the imbiber into a Theta state, effecting healing often with purging, inducing visions and giving access to insight and understanding.
Within many different cultures Shaman have accessed these states through the use of what they would call sacred teaching plants. These are sometimes referred to as drugs in our culture and consumed in a disrespectful way that does not necessarily yield a positive result. When these teaching plants are taken within the proper context and with the intent to learn and understand they can provide powerful lessons and teaching. The plants induce a similar state that could otherwise be entered through meditative visualisation. Ingesting the teaching plant is similar to taking a high-speed journey into a specific state with a certain

amount of chaos present. Meditative visualisation is more like moving slowly and carefully in that direction. When we use visualisation we are invoking the power of our imagination in a capacity that calls on all of our senses to assist, somewhat like the description Einstein gave of using his visual and feeling sense. We commence by imagining and similarly to Einstein need to establish parameters whereby we can rigorously test our results, to establish the truth. We embark on a series of experiments in order to test our capacity to work beyond the physical. I have heard it said that the teaching plants are a window not a doorway.

Out of body experiences, remote viewing, powerful healings, reports of spiritual encounters are all associated with the Theta state. The Shaman understands that the Theta state is akin to the spirit realm. So seeks this resonance in order to communicate with spirits directly. The shaman seeks to navigate this other reality, or dreaming state, both with care and understanding. In a synchronous way we may well encounter one off experiences, where we have moved into this type of state, yet the Shaman seeks to consciously move between these states, between these worlds for the benefit of others.

THE TRANSPERSONAL AND THE SHAMAN

Within the discipline of psychology, the study of the mind and mental health, we find a development of ideas starting from the founder of this field Sigmund Freud who coined the term psychoanalysis in 1896 and mostly explored ideas of the unconscious.
Jung, Freud's contemporary developed the concept of the collective unconscious and archetypes in 1916.

What developed next, was considered a more scientific approach, called behaviourism, which centred around information largely taken from the study of animal behaviours, this became the prevalent paradigm during 1920's-1950's
In 1958, on the back of a dawning recognition that the scope of the human psyche was broader than psychoanalysis and behaviourism allowed, Abraham Maslow ushered in a third approach he called Humanistic Psychology. This focused on the human psyche rather than the study of animal behaviour (rats and pigeons), and went further than looking at base instinct and pathology.
Maslow was interested in peak experiences and through studying peak

experiences, expanded his view of the spectrum of experiences that human beings were capable of and in so doing had to expand the scientific paradigm to be able to look at and work effectively with these other states. Maslow describes peak experience as:

"rare, exciting, oceanic, deeply moving, exhilarating, elevating experiences that generate an advanced form of perceiving reality, and are even mystic and magical in their effect upon the experimenter." Maslow 1964

And later;

"It has begun to appear strongly that this phenomena (peak experience) is a diluted, more secular, more frequent version of the mystical experience that has been described so often as to have become what Huxley calls *The perennial Philosophy*. In various cultures and in various eras it takes on somewhat different coloration-and yet its essence is always recognizable –it is the same."   Maslow 1973 p64

As the 1960's progressed, Maslow together with Stanislav Grof and others went on to develop Transpersonal psychology this took form by by 1968.
Meanwhile Roberto Assagioli, the father of Psychosynthesis, who had been working in Italy since 1926 with a model that incorporated the spiritual dimension, immediately took up the term Transpersonal.
The term Transpersonal refers to aspects of experience beyond the personal, as in Maslow's peak experiences, and aspects of Grof's work that allowed people to experience universal expansive feelings that took them beyond the identification with only their personal self. This allowed experiences of deep universal connection to be seen as part of human psychology, rather than necessarily as some kind of breakdown or pathology.
Interestingly this brings the model of psychotherapy more in line with the ancient Shamanic view and with the view of many religions and philosophies.
More and more techniques are being introduced that use the imagination and visualisation to re-program the sub-conscious and reshape or reframe past experience in order to affect a persons present state. These techniques are also used to develop inner resources and insight even to accomplish future goals.
This is not a new development in psychotherapy as Jung used these

methods during his life time. In Memories Dreams and reflections, published after his death, there are accounts of both Jung's visualisation experiments and some of the spontaneous visions he had after his heart attack, with characters that could be called architypes or 'spirit guides'. Jung attributed some of his greatest ideas to one of his Spirit guides, Philemon who he encountered in his 30's during his visualisation experiments. During his experiments he met with two guides Elijah and Salome, Elijah later changed into Philemon, it was with them that he discussed and discovered various of the ideas that have shaped psychotherapy today.

Here is one of his experiments in which he experiences the stripping away of his identification with him-self.

"Something new entered my field of vision. A short distance away I saw in space a tremendous dark block of stone, like a meteorite. It was about the size of my house, or even bigger. It was floating in space, and I myself was floating in space.

An entrance led into a small antechamber. To the right of the entrance, a black Hindu sat silently in lotus posture upon a stone bench…I knew that he expected me. Two steps led up to this antechamber, and inside…was the gate to the temple. As I approached the steps leading up to the entrance into the rock, a strange thing happened: I had the feeling that everything was being sloughed away; everything I aimed at or wished for or thought, the whole phantasmagoria of earthly existence, fell away or was stripped from me---an extremely painful process. Nevertheless something remained; it was as if I now carried along with me everything I had ever experienced or done, everything that had happened around me. I might also say: it was with me, and I was it. I consisted of all that, so to speak. I consisted of my own history, and I felt with great certainty: this is what I am. I am this bundle of what has been, and what has been accomplished. This experience gave me a feeling of extreme poverty, but at the same time of great fullness."

These kinds of experiences and communications with spirit guides are a major component of the Shamanic approach and I was amazed and delighted to discover that at the roots of psychotherapy, there was a spontaneous connection with the spirit realm through the experiments and experiences of Jung.

THE POWER OF THE HEART

"Each pulsing beat of the heart, in fact, produces two-and-a-half watts of electrical energy. And this electrical charge, though pulsating, is continuous, just as the heart, throughout life is continuous in its beating. It is this pattern of electrical activity that is measured when an electrocardiogram (ECG) is taken by placing electrodes on the body. But the heart also generates magnetic fields (which is why it is often referred to as electromagnetic, instead of just electric) and those magnetic fields can be measured as well, with a magnetocardiogram."

Stefan Harrod Buhner, The secret life of plants Page 86

What needs to be included here is what occurs when the mind and heart are working together. Since the development of digital EEG machines researchers have discovered much higher speeds at which the brain can function above the 25 Hz of the Beta state. This has been called Gamma and ranges from 40-100 Hz. This has largely been encountered amongst Buddhist monks and Nuns practising loving kindness meditations. When we consider the electromagnetic energy in the brain is operating at a far lower wattage than the electromagnetic energy of the heart, we should not be surprised that something powerful occurs when the brain and heart are synchronised. Visualisation is a major part of loving kindness meditations, that develop compassion, firstly; for those we love and then progressively moving towards those we do not. The mind is directing the heart to feel love. This can also be experienced when we give thanks, reaching out with the heart and mind to touch all the things that support life. This action can significantly change the way in which nature responds to our presence. Not only that, but also how people respond to us.

Researcher has found that the Gamma state of around 40 Hz unifies both hemispheres of the brain; creates a feeling of bliss, supports mental sharpness, and fast memory recall.

I hypothesise that the syncronising of the heart with the mind amplifies the brainwave state, and steps it up to the Gama speed. We are using the Theta brainwave state when we visualize between 4-8 Hz so if this is amplified by 10 we get into the Gama range.

Accessing the Gamma state using scientific or shamanic methods that do not rely on entrainment require both imagining/visualisation and generating feelings of love. This illustrates the importance of harnessing the power of the heart when we transition into other states. It is the heart that empowers these experiences quite literally.

CHAPTER 5

WARRIOR OF THE HEART

ATTITUDE OF THE WARRIOR QUALITIES OF THE CHILD

"Discipline, as understood by a warrior, is creative, open, and produces freedom. It is the ability to face the unknown, transforming the feeling of knowing into reverent astonishment; of considering things that exceed the scope of our habits, and daring to face the only war that is worthwhile: The battle for awareness."
~ Carlos Castaneda

"Budo is not the felling of an opponent by force; nor is it a tool to lead the world to destruction with arms. True Budo is to accept the spirit of the universe, keep the peace of the world, correctly produce, protect and cultivate all beings in nature."

Morihei Ueshiba The way of peace

We were sitting in Vondle Park in Amsterdam enjoying the afternoon sun. I sat with my back to a tree while my girlfriend sat opposite. We shared a bottle of wine and each other's company. Some drummers were jamming a short distance away adding to the relaxed atmosphere. Towards the lake there was a large pile of pollarded tree limbs. Quite suddenly all the ducks that were floating on the lake took to the air. It was at this point that I began to feel wary what was coming that had so effectively cleared the lake of birds. We observed a man coming our way; he was unshaven and roughly dressed. He took a large piece of cut timber from the pile of branches and began whacking the trees with full force as he made his way towards us. As other walkers looked at him he cursed at them and the park began to quickly clear of humans as well as ducks. As I lay with my back to the tree I felt determined that I was not going to let "my" tree get whacked. The man came closer, the drummers looked at him and his curse encrusted answer to their affront of looking at him, sent them packing. We remained seeing this man literally on the rampage and we were in his path. We both looked at him, I felt filled with compassion for this ravaged man and began on the spot to send him love. He came up to us and we unflinchingly gazed at him. We locked in and he crouched down and began to dig his stick into the ground as if he wanted to hurt the earth. He spat out his story, which was so charged with cursing that I found it hard to understand the sense of what he told. He would break my gaze to swear at passes by who looked at him in awe and fear. As he shared and we tried to receive him he began to soften, my girlfriend offered him some of the wine we were drinking in a gesture of companionship. He calmed right down. We began to piece together his story of paranoia and pain. We discovered in the end that he was hungry and offered him some money for food. Later we passed him getting some chips from a nearby chip van.

Two days later someone tried to mug me in broad daylight. It was one of those situations you know you could have avoided. I was in the red-light district carrying my back pack intending to leave town that night. A guy leaning up against the corner of an ally way called out "Want a ten Guilders deal?" "No thanks", was my response, I had spent the morning clearing my head in the park with some training and meditation. At the end of which I had put a five Guilders note in my top pocket separate from the rest of my money.

"Come over here I just want to talk to you" He said, his tone had softened and my defences came down. What harm could come from talking, I thought. I went over to see what was up. He grabbed the shoulder strap of my bag containing the majority of my money, camera, passport etc.. and dragged me into the alley he was on the corner of.

With knife in hand he said "Give me all your money". I was shocked and found myself thinking that if I gave him all of my money I would have to return home and it was day three of a month's holiday in Europe for me and my brother. "I have not got any money" I replied. We were rapidly approaching a stalemate. Either he needed to scare me more, by being more threatening or I could try to run, this was impossible as he had hold of my bag that had all my money in it and I had my rucksack on too. The other option was for me to hit him. He started to go through my pockets. Revealing train timetables tourist information and other useless stuff. It was at this point that I remembered the 5 guilders note. I pulled it out and offered it to him. "This is all the money I have" I lied. At this point he looked at me as if I had insulted his mother. In disgust and desperation, he put the money back in my top pocket. "It was a joke" he said and sat down on the step behind him. I was confused, it had not been a joke, and I wondered whether to talk to him about what had happened. Yet I also felt that it was time to leave the area quickly. So I did. Heading for the front of the station, where I was going to meet my brother and head out of Amsterdam on the next train to Portugal. It was only afterwards that the adrenaline kicked in and with it the paranoia. I suddenly felt vulnerable; everyone around me became a possible attacker, someone out to get one over on me.

It was late in the afternoon that I noticed him, the dishevelled man who had created the disturbance in Vondle Park two days before. We caught each-others eye and we said hello. He seemed to be in a worse state. "I've got a piece of glass in my pocket and I am going to kill someone" was what he told me in confidence. His voice filled with passionate anger. For my part when confronted with this challenging situation my own feelings of paranoia and fear dissipated. I tried to understand why he felt this way. Eventually I managed to encourage him to put the piece of glass in a nearby bin. I also gave him the remainder of my guilders in coins as they were going to be of no use to me as soon as I left Amsterdam.

After this strange meeting I felt more in control of my own state boarding the train a few hours later and finally meeting my brother to continue the journey.

THOMAS SCHORR-KON

ATTITUDE OF THE WARRIOR PEACEMAKER

"Live with a peaceful heart; cultivate a warrior's spirit. "

Dan Millman Way of the peaceful warrior

The purpose of the warrior's attitude is that it helps us develop the capacity to deal with difficult and challenging situations, to relate to reality clearly. It encourages us to seek harmony rather than conflict through tempering our physical and emotional states. Ultimately helping us to move into a state beyond defense, beyond self-identification and the separation this reinforces.

"You haven't yet opened your heart fully, to life, to each moment. The peaceful warrior's way is not about invulnerability, but absolute vulnerability--to the world, to life…… All along I've shown you by example that a warrior's life is not about imagined perfection or victory; it is about love. Love is a warrior's sword; wherever it cuts, it gives life, not death." Dan Millman Way of the peaceful warrior

The concept of warriorship is found in most cultures and perhaps seems obsolete and even dangerous model as it is currently portrayed in the movies we see. These caricatured versions of the hero's journey serve only to distort aspects of genuine warriorship often portraying violence, revenge and callousness as the qualities to be lauded.

Yet there are innate associations and instinctive aspects of our psyche bound up with warriorship. As children we play out these roles and many of the real aspects of warriorship are key philosophical principles that can help us live vibrant and fulfilled lives.

When we explore the context of how warriorship is expressed in Zen and Tibetan Buddhism, the martial arts and shamanism we discover that it is closer to peace-making than the perpetuation of violence. Firstly it is neither overly aggressive nor flimsy. It involves a great deal of sensitivity and self-knowledge. It requires the courage to open ourselves up and let the light of day shine in on all the murky corners that we do not feel are worthy aspects of ourselves. Through this process we discover that the fundamental ground of our being is good. That all of the aspects of ourselves are there for a purpose and are integral. That within each perceived negative there is the possibility to develop the positive, or develop the right relationship to the negative. It is a practice that centres on the heart. It comes down to the recognition that the only battle is with the self. The overcoming of the way the mind conflicts with itself, the very quieting of the mind and the confronting of fear. It is through the necessity for these internal conditions within a battlefield circumstance that they have become associated with the warrior. To get caught up in internal struggles of any kind draws our attention away from the moment. On the battlefield this will lead to death.

Looking at warriorship as a practice and metaphor we have to redefine the myths that surround this term in order to understand that its real power comes from the principle of softness. There will always be someone harder than you but not necessarily someone softer. So the combination of softness and yielding in order to advance becomes a very powerful combination. This is likened to water.

"Become like water my friend". Bruce Lee

There are a number of principles that underlie all forms of movement the discovery of which helps us understand how to organise the body in a powerful way, relying on the innate strength of our structure. The beauty of principles is that we can extrapolate information from them rather than needing everything to be spelled out. We also discover that they often relate to far more than the single context in which they are taught.

As an example if we take the principle of softness; by just softening the body in the face of a conflict situation, physically we will be able to act and react much more quickly with a relaxed body. Any actions will utilise the body's power far more efficiently.

Remaining soft in the face of aggression is counterintuitive as the normal response is to tense and make ready for fight or flight. The secondary effect of this response is that the aggressor perceives the relaxed response in several different ways. The relaxed response tends to create a calming effect both because the reaction that is expected or provoked is not there, so there is no engagement in the dynamic of escalation of aggression. Acting in this way requires a level of emotional self-mastery. The body language signal this sends tends to be unnerving for the aggressor and demonstrates the mood of the warrior.

The relaxed response is very hard to read, if the aggressor is intent on attack, tension in any part of the body disrupts grounding so upper body tension for example will make a person more unstable. If we are able to soften then we have overcome 50% of the aggression in the situation by dealing with our own reaction, skilfully. How we relate to our thoughts and our emotions determines how much freedom and real choice we have.

Our relationship to fear is the key to our capacity to move beyond tension and develop softness. This is the real battle that the warrior is dealing with reducing and relaxing self-conflict, we are the opponent we need to master. Hence warriorship turns out to be about the journey towards self-mastery or understanding the self.

As we work in nature we discover that nature reflects our attitude back to us unconditionally. If we are projecting fear or thanksgiving we will get it back, our attitude in a survival situation determines whether we survive or not. It makes the difference between dangerous struggle, survival or coming home.

The attitude of the warrior is also central to the practice of shamanism and experiential spiritual development as it provides strategies to see the self clearly and in difficult times aids in the realignment of the self; helping us relate to the vastness and mystery of the universe and the paradoxes of the various realms we inhabit, in a workable and powerful way.

Warriorship also has a role in helping to integrate youthful exuberant energy, especially masculine energy, which our current society being so civilised does not seem to know what to do with. As our gender roles are shifting young men are finding it hard to integrate their explosive power whereas in times past the hunt was a vehicle for tempering these energies; from the silent skills of stalking and careful observation of the prey to the sacred act of taking life. The tradition of becoming a man in many Earth based societies was bound up with the killing of a powerful animal for the benefit of the tribe. This act has the capacity to bring understanding to the young man, that what life offers us, is in the gift of the greater forces of nature and spirit. The key for the young person is in their capacity to align themselves with these forces not to master or dominate them.

Rites of passage are an important part of becoming ourselves, whether it is us moving into our gender identity, being born into the wider realms of spirit and nature, or connecting to and understanding our vision and purpose.

The expansive powerful energy that we often feel as children and young adults, the expression of our feelings of being very much alive, are what is at stake here. Often we are schooled out of accessing this quality of energy. Yet through the qualities of the child we can access this aliveness, and have the possibility to unlearn enough to free up our energy and passion. Often this is accomplished through play. We also discover there are many other aspects that we have lost from our childhood, such as our ability to be fully in the present, our inquisitiveness, our rapture, our ability to become so absorbed in what we are doing that all distraction is removed. When these qualities are tapped into and integrated consciously there is a dialogue between our child and adult selves and a capacity to reincorporate the gifts of the child into our daily experience with a maturity that brings great spontaneity and tenderness into the moment.

THOMAS SCHORR-KON

HIGHEST FORM OF MARTIAL ARTS
THE WAY OF THE PEACEMAKER

"The ultimate aim of martial arts is not having to use them"

Miyamoto Musashi, A book of five rings

Martial arts practice can take many years to master and is always trying to push the practitioner out of their comfort zone to expanding their capacity, energy and skill. When I started training my first karate instructor Sensei Terry Dukes or Nagaboshi Tonio as he was later known, told me if I got into a fight I would be thrown out of the Dojo. So I began with the attitude of training so I did not have to fight. This developed power and resilience affording more choices in the face of difficulty. Developing the energy necessary to be fully present in the face of danger and creating the understanding that fighting is an absolute last resort. This led with many more years of training to recognising that even self-defence may be an intrinsically violent attitude and finally coming to the understanding that the highest form of martial art is to have the inner strength not to fight, but to reach out with the heart.

There is a beautiful account of a third-degree Aikido black-belt who was training in Japan. To achieve a third-degree takes upwards of 30 years of training and this practitioner had trained in a righteous fashion. Always trying to avoid trouble, he believed that one day he would use his skills to defend the weak against the strong. As he rode on a crowded underground train, a drunken Japanese workman got on board, knocking over a mother and child. The Aikido man thought now is my chance, and he stood up to draw the workman's attention." I'll teach you some Japanese manners" the drunken workmen shouted as he lurched towards the Aikido player. As he stood there he thought "the moment he touches me I'll drop in his socks". He hadn't noticed an immaculately dressed older Japanese fellow sat next to him. As the workman lurched towards him this Japanese man called out "Hey" as if the workman was his long lost friend. He continued "Ah you've been drinking, how nice, I like a drink, especially when I return from work,. I usually drink some sake in the garden with my wife, under the persimmon tree. We only got two persimmon's last year." By this time the workman had sat in the seat opposite his head in his hands and began to weep. "I had a wife and a job……" It was at this point that the Aikido man felt like a piece of shit for what he had attempted to do with his martial arts skill of over 30 years the old man next to him had accomplished with a few kind words.

This is an example of the highest form of martial arts, reaching out with the heart and not lifting a finger. This is true Warriorship and comes with the understanding that people in pain do painful things. When we relate to a person's pain rather than their aggression we have the capacity to transform the situation by meeting their pain. We don't even need to speak out loud if our compassionate heart is engaged fearlessly.

By finding a point of connection for example 'Ah brother you've been drinking, I like a drink too sometimes'. We can meet their heart and recognise that it is only pain that creates aggression. What they are seeking is to express their pain. They however are not concerned as to how this is expressed or accommodated. It could be by them attacking you or by you hurting them, either outcome is a way they can feel their pain. This perpetuates more pain. Yet if we remain centred and able to work with our heart in the face of aggression the situation can shift so they may be able to feel their emotional pain and express that rather than it being expressed as aggression and violence and cause more suffering.

If this is not possible, then if we can manage to overcome the adrenal response in us we can remain in a state of maximum choice and still act rather than be thrown into a state of reaction. It is in this arena that the real warrior fights his or her battles, as to overcome the reactive self is to remain present. The main battle the warrior faces is with the self. This is both in remaining centred emotionally in relation to external events and internally in reducing the capacity of the mind to conflict with itself. This stands us in good stead in any situation.

There are no contests in the Art of Peace. A true warrior is invincible because he or she contests with nothing. Defeat means to defeat the mind of contention that we harbor within.   Morihei Ueshiba

I have witnessed several times the shift that occurs in a person who is experiencing the diminishment of choice and moving towards the fight response. Firstly they lose the capacity to reason, or more pointedly you lose the capacity to reason with them. Then the red mist comes down, this can be seen in their eyes. They have at this point nearly lost control of themselves; as far as a warrior is concerned at this point they have lost. The aggressor is at this point looking to justify their position in order to feel righteous enough to attack. It is still possible to try to re-humanise the situation in order to calm your opponent down. Personally if a fight occurs I consider I have lost, whatever the outcome of the fight.

We had been staying in the flat belonging to my partners ex he had kindly offered it to us while my partner ran a trade show in London. After the show he returned. I suggested to my partner that we leave out of respect, and she said that she would ask if it was alright for us to stay on for a few more days. Her ex-partner said yes but did not mean it. That night he got very drunk. Before he kicked off my partner sensed this was going to happen and left the flat. So when he started to try to argue with me about my treatment of his son, my step son and paying him for staying in the flat sums of money that made me realise he was out of control. He was seeking to find a way to feel righteous in order to attack me. I tried to leave but he blocked my way. He is a big man and had beaten up two previous ex-partners hospitalising one of them. He had also attacked his ex-partner as well in the past, so he had form. I tried to re-humanise the situation by making a cup of tea in the kitchen and offering him one. By this time the red mist had come down in his eyes and I realised if a fight broke out it would have serious repercussions. How it would affect his son, how we would smash up the small flat. How my main recourse would be a strike to the throat, a possible killing strike. There was no option to fight in my mind just a reduction of aggression until calm could be restored. I eventually called the police, who seemed non-plused by my description of events.

This triggered a response of him taking the dog out. At this point I left too. He later told my partner that my martial are skills were rubbish. This delighted me as we had been in the flat for 45 minutes and he had not been able to attack me. He had just had a masterclass in not fighting, the highest form of martial arts and had not even realised.

MOOD OF THE WARRIOR

"'One needs the mood of a warrior for every single act,' he said. 'Otherwise one becomes distorted and ugly. There is no power in a life that lacks this mood. Look at yourself. Everything offends and upsets you. You whine and complain and feel that everyone is making you dance to their tune. You are a leaf at the mercy of the wind. There is no power in your life. What an ugly feeling that must be. 'A warrior on the other hand, is a hunter. He calculates everything. That's control. But once his calculations are over, he acts. He lets go. That's abandon. A warrior is not a leaf at the mercy of the wind. No one can push him: no one can make him do things against himself or against his better judgement. A warrior is tuned to survive, and he survives in the best of all possible fashions.' "

Carlos Castaneda Journey to Ixtlan p135

The mood of the warrior as described by Castaneda puts forward a state of inner preparedness. It involves choices that have been made before the situation arises that are at the root of the survival attitude, choices that also stands us in good stead in any other aspect of life. We are not overwhelmed by or fighting against nature we are returning home, moving towards oneness.

The mood of the warrior or peacemaker is bound up with fearlessly being oneself. It is a choice, underlying it may be various strategies, yet it rests on our capacity to create a warm hearted, resilient and centred state wherever we are whatever our day looks like. It is helpful for us to explore further some of the attributes of the warrior in order to get a clear picture of how this is possible.

"Everything can be taken from a man but one thing: the last of human freedoms- to choose ones attitude in any given set of circumstances, to choose one's own way." Viktor E. Frankl

The type of warrior I refer to here is tempered; the last to pick up the lance, there is no desire for conflict or aversion to it. Because enough attention and presence has been paid to the warriors own inner conflicts, and feelings, most often through meditation and reflection. Coupled with a careful look at the roots of violence both in ourselves and in others, seeing how separation and not feeling loved enough creates pain and suffering and then is expressed as aggression.

The warrior is engaged in seeking harmony, this is not in an attempt to please others or with the sacrifice of awareness or sensitivity. The main perspective is of resting in a state of being robustly present, from this state conflict can skilfully be dissolved. There is also recognition that celebrating the journey is the main discipline. The mood of the warrior is a dance between intent and surrender, the calculation is akinto setting the intent and abandonment is the surrender. The warrior's mood is a form of skilful action and is tuned by being curious about whatever arises rather than judgemental. So if aggression or joy arises it does not cause concern, it is just related to skilfully.

"As soon as you concern yourself with the 'good' and 'bad' of your fellows, you create an opening in your heart for maliciousness to enter. Testing, competing with, and criticizing others weaken and defeat you."

Morihei Ueshiba

"Allow rather than resist what arises in the present moment-inside or out. Let it be interesting rather than good or bad."

Dan Millman- The way of the peaceful warrior.

This is crucial because we cannot know what is good and bad we can only hold a limited opinion which may change as time passes. In The water course way Alan Watts recounts a story of a Taoist whose horse runs away and it becomes clear that the interpretation of events can change at every turn:

"That evening the neighbours gathered to commiserate with him since this was such bad luck. He said, 'May be.' The next day the horse returned, but brought with it six wild horses, and the neighbours came exclaiming at his good fortune. He said, 'May be.' And then, the following day, his son tried to saddle and ride one of the wild horses, was thrown, and broke his leg. Again the neighbours came to offer their sympathy for the misfortune. He said, 'May be.' The day after that, conscription officers came to the village to seize young men for the army, but because of the broken leg the farmer's son was rejected. When the neighbours came into say how fortunately everything had turned out, he said, 'May be.'"

Alan Watts, The watercourse way

We just don't know what is good and bad so if we skilluly relate to the situation with curiosity we can remain free of judgement, not only that we can help those around us to relate to their situations more clearly by not taking sides. When our default position is to seek to learn from the difficult experiences we have and see for example what the person we are finding annoying is reflecting back to us about ourselves. We can relate to what is happening, rather than reacting to continuous judgement.

TERRITORY AND DEFENSE

The habit of being defensive at its roots grows from a sense of separation. As social creatures humans create groups that grow into tribes even nations. These divisions are then fiercely defended. The separation with nature and the alienation of the general populace from the Earth largely through economic progress is also a huge form of violence.

"When you call yourself an Indian or a Muslim Christian or a European, or anything else, you're being violent. Do you see why it is violent? Because you are separating yourself from the rest of mankind. When you separate yourself by belief, by nationality, by tradition, it breeds violence. So a man who is seeking to understand violence does not belong to any country, to any religion, to any political party or partial system; he is concerned with the total understanding of mankind."   J Krishnamurti

When we create separations we create territories that need to be defended. It is as if the main disease of our current culture is based on separation, separation from self, from each other and from nature. I have found that defence is the worst defence, because it is in essence an aggressive stance. It is a posture against other, and protective of a separate self. If on the other hand our intention is to yield in order to advance and we recognise that if we are truly involved in self-defence we are always going to be late (i.e. not the first to make a move) we can relax into the moment.

When we consider that any form of separation is merely an idea and that we cannot exist without the wider community of air, water, earth and fire. Perhaps this will affect our perspective in relation to defence.

Unfortunately these ideas of separation are deeply rooted in our physical minds, and seeing through this, and letting go of it can only occur once we have peeled ourselves away from the extremely sticky nature of thought, allowing more space between us and our thinking. Perhaps through the practice of meditation or the steady mind or some form of movement practice.

Krishnamurti's perspective is illuminating from an ultimate perspective, helping us understand the underlying cause of violence, yet in our day to day experience we may need to maintain certain boundaries until we fully realise the meaning of oneness and move entirely into the heart of vulnerability. At this point we do not need boundaries anymore..

"Oneness does not mean we are all the same." Adyashanti

Personally I chose to look at this type of situation as if there is an imperative to love everyone but that does not mean I have to like everyone i.e. there is an under lying unity expressed yet there may be personal preferences for certain behaviours like integrity, honesty, kindness etc that I choose and prefer to be around. We are all unique and our journey to awakening is unique, there is no formula, just pointers.

"Wake up! Wake up! Soon the person you believe you are will die - so now, wake up and be content with this knowledge: there is no need to search; achievement leads to nowhere. It makes no difference at all, so just be happy now! Love is the only reality of the world, because it is all ONE, you see. And the only laws are paradox, humor, and change. There is no problem, never was, and never will be. Release your struggle, let go of your mind, throw away your concerns, and relax into the world. No need to resist life; just do your best. Open your eyes and see that you are far more than you imagine. you are the world, you are the universe; you are yourself and everyone else too! It's all the marvelous Play of God. Wake up, regain your humor. Don't worry, just be happy. You are already free!"

Dan Millman-Way of the peaceful warrior.

FIGHT OR FLIGHT

Choice is crucial here, if we are forced into an emotional corner, then it feels as if our choices are limited. Often this results in the expression of anger when the underlying emotion could well be that of sadness. It may be that our incapacity to courageously express our boundaries is the cause of this sadness, and we think that by displaying anger we can win back the ground we feel we have lost. That is not to say that the expression of anger does not have a place, but as we become physically or emotionally powerful we need to be responsible around our expression of intense emotion. I have found that all the anger I have expressed was always anger at the self. Anger is also like taking poison and expecting it to affect your enemy.

If on the other hand we are able to be vulnerable and experience our sadness in the moment, it may be possible for us to be understood without aggression.

Having the courage to remain relaxed and vulnerable, we retain infinity of choice in our responses. It is a level of sensitivity that is not disrupted by other people's aggression. As if we are treasuring or savouring this quality not just for our own sanity but for all those we meet. Our sensitivity when integrated with courage becomes very powerful because we are more able to turn on the head of a pin rather than be crushed by personal remarks. This is the development of emotional resilience.

To maintain this in the face of aggression demands the Warriors level of courage, when this is achieved we truly become peacemakers. This is because we are not forced into the diminished position of fight, flight, freeze, appease or collapse, our options remain open and our capacity to choose a movement towards a peaceful resolution rather than an explosive reaction is far more likely.

The diminishment of our responses is called our survival instinct i.e. fight or flight etc What is revealed to us in the martial arts and the development of stalking skills is that counterintuitive responses are often far more useful than our instinctive response. It is possible for us to connect with and harness these deeply rooted survival instincts and use them for our benefit if all other choices are removed.

So these survival instincts are important to us, we are not trying to override them we are trying to harness them and temper them and this creates more choices in difficult circumstances. So our survival instinct remains primal and highly tuned but it becomes at our disposal and within the realms of conscious choice rather than it being triggered and taking over our state. To achieve this we need to have processed many confrontational situations (this can occur to some degree in the dojo when training) and then observe our reactions, working overtime to reroute the adrenalin response so we can use the energy it provides or at least diminish the disruption it can cause to the system.

It is the release of adrenalin that floods our system that can diminish our choice, when we can assimilate the adrenaline quickly we can return to a broader place of choice. Chemically we see that when the body is more alkaline the adrenaline can be repurposed. The simplest way to alkalise the body is through bringing more oxygen into the blood, as oxygen is alkaline and carbon dioxide is acidic. So by exercising and breathing more we create a better environment in the body for the utilising of adrenaline.

When we consider the idea that separation breeds violence this may well impact on our concept of self-defence. This could move us towards an understanding that openheartedness though appearing softer demands far greater courage than trying to defend ourselves and leads us to a perspective of seeking harmony. It is defensiveness and aggression created by separation that we are seeking to diffuse and heal. When we combine this with the recognition that people in pain do painful things then our attention moves from their aggressive behaviour to the pain that motivates their actions. By meeting the pain rather than reacting to the expression of violence we make a shift that allows the type of compassionate and courageous act that forms the basis of the story of the Aikido man on the train in Japan above. This story illustrates the Aikido man's reaction to the violence of the workman, and genuine warriorship displayed by the Japanese man meeting the workman's pain with his kind words. It is as if the softness and tempering of the heart are an expression of a childlike quality, the quality of vulnerability. If we slightly redefine the term childlike to unconditioned, then we start to see how vulnerability is very much about a stripping away of our defensive layers. When we express vulnerability we build trust and connection.

The reduction of our ability to respond, to a handful of reactions diminishes what is in effect our response ability. Ability to respond and responsibility are very much the same.

If we are 'like a leaf blown in the wind', then we have no power. Carlos Castaneda's allusion suggests that if we are blaming external circumstances for our condition then we are not taking responsibility for ourselves and our feelings.

As we take responsibility we beginto become empowered. If you have power you must act responsibly, if you accept responsibility you can act powerfully. Power equals responsibility and accepting responsibility equals power to act.

This means that if we take responsibility for the situation, even if it appears to be beyond our control or not our fault we put ourselves in a position to do something about it. We shift from having something done to us and a victim mentality, to being able to act. We are transforming our reaction into action.

Having said this there are many experiences in life that can provoke reactions to become lodged in the mind or body that emerge before we are able to consciously choose a path of action. How we undo this is a vital part of the journey. Often in relating skilfully to our own difficulties we grow in our compassion for others.

A clear example in survival training of being able to take responsibility is the information of the survival priorities. Merely knowing the order of survival priorities gives us a sense of how to take care of ourselves in an unknown wilderness situation and therefore protects us from falling into despondency or taking the wrong action. We have already decided that the situation is workable and understand how to proceed. The warrior has made a calculation, a strategy and all that is left to do is to act.

GRIEF AND PRAISE

Martine Prechtel in his book "The small of rain on dust" eloquently talks about the process of transforming grief to praise, reminding us that if our communities and social structures no longer have the capacity to hold our grief, then we need to seek the wider community of nature to be able to fully express our grief and help it turn to praise for what we have loved and lost.

"No matter what kind of person goes to the sea to grieve, we must have people to help us when we are in this place. Even if we are not capable of being in grief, or we think we can handle it ourselves, we need people to help us grieve as best we can even if we are not yet good at it. This is no race or competition, but a natural function, a gift from life to make life livable again, for those who would live life all the way: those who fall in love. You might expect that, after 2.000 or 3,000 years of repression and a culturally endorsed incapacity with grief, most individuals would be totally inept at letting grief roll out onto the beach to the mother of us all: the salty ocean. But it usually comes as a great surprise and relief how naturally people grieve when it is safe to do so. So we need the ocean and a friend."

Martine Prechtel The small of rain on dust page 51

Experiencing this grief is part of the Warriors heart, and is the equivalent of a kind of intimacy with the past, the Earth and our ancestors. We cannot allow this to overwhelm or undermine us but harness it to help to motivate us to see clearly how we have got to where we are and move compassionately forwards.

As Stephen Jenkinson says 'grief is a skill', and our capacity to tend our grief and the grief of others is something we need to develop the ability to encompass. This grief holds within it our fear of death, the fear that underpins all other fear, how we relate to this in ourselves is crucial for our lives.

Tom Brown Jr's story of grandfather and the fishermen expresses with power this issue. Do we choose to truly live, with vitality and rapture or do we choose to be like the living dead hiding from life, never truly having lived. Because living without vitality and rapture without courage is what causes us the greatest grief at the end of our lives.

What starts to become clear is that our ability to act is determined more by our internal process than external events. When we can hold both the grief of loss and the joy every moment brings in our hearts simultaneously our hearts become strong and resilient. It produces a powerful softness that is humble and full, a heartfullness.

FEAR AND FEARLESSNESS

The fearless warrior is not taking things personally, and is moving through fear whenever it arises, i.e. acting fearlessly. Understanding that the fear of death underpins all fear, the warrior has an acceptance of death as a certainty and no hurry towards it. Because of this, she or he is open and heartfelt, courageous in the true meaning of the word.

The word courage comes from the old French for heart (coeur), the etymological meaning of courage is tempered innermost feelings. It is this tempering of the heart and emotions that brings gentleness. When a steel blade is made it is first hardened, so the edge can be made extremely sharp. The tempering part of the process softens the metal so that it is not too brittle and does not shatter. The phrase to lose your temper is a metaphoric expression of this brittleness which is an emotional aspect that needs to be tempered with a soft heart.

"For the warrior, this experience of sad and tender heart is what gives birth to fearlessness. Conventionally, being fearless means that you are not afraid or that, if someone hits you, you will hit them back. However, we are not talking about that street-fighter level of fearlessness. Real fearlessness is the product of tenderness. It comes from letting the world tickle your heart, your raw and beautiful heart. You are willing to open up, without resistance or shyness, and face the world. You are willing to share your heart with others."

Shambala, (The sacred path of the warrior), Chogyam Trungpa.

Fear reduces our capacity to respond, it reduces our responses down to 5 basic reactions: fight, flight, freeze, appease or collapse. When we develop the capacity to move towards fear in order to understand it and watch it change, we are developing the capacity to process emotions more swiftly. When we get curious about our fear, wanting to know where it comes from, what creates it, our relationship to it changes and we beginto make an investigation into where we find fear in our lives. We start to greet it is an old friend, knowing it well. This is the beginning of developing courage and moving beyond fear, because we find that in every corner of our life there is the spectre of fear. We have our work cut out for us to pay attention to this in order to start to live fully. Through the process of engaging with our fear we develop the capacity to relate to all the other so called negative emotions. The moment we choose fear as our greatest teacher we are firmly on the path of the warrior.

"To be free from the fear of death does not mean pretending to oneself in one's good hours, that one will not tremble in the face of death, and that there is nothing to fear. Rather, he who masters both life and death is free from fear of any kind to the extent that he is no longer capable of experiencing what fear feels like. Those who do not know the power of rigorous and protracted meditation cannot judge of the self-conquest it makes possible. At any rate the perfected master betrays his fearlessness at every turn, not in words, but in his whole demeanour: one has only to look at him to be profoundly affected by it. Unshakable fearlessness as such already amounts to mastery, which in the nature of things is only realized by the few."

P104 Zen and the art of archery

A genuine kind of authenticity is revealed when we are able to process our fear daily. Our tendency for our emotions to get stuck is diminished. We can let go of recreating past trauma from painful events that can stretch back to our childhoods, by bringing our sensitivity and spaciousness to the present moment. We can unravel our emotional responses and fear is an excellent indicator of something we need to bring our attention to. When we start to transform our fear or any difficult emotion we are meeting the principle that whatever we perceive to be the problem is the next thing to deal with. We are developing our emotion into a skill, an action. Eventually being able to choose our emotional state as in the mood of the warrior.

This process demands a level of honesty with the self, it is this level of truthfulness with ourselves that is a foundational aspect of the warrior.

We can only genuinely be open and honest if we start with the self. We are trying to perceive reality clearly and truth helps us become both authentic and relate directly to reality.

In my own experience as a man, the first place that I have encountered fear is between me and other men. It starts as boys and develops into a full-blown antler clashing, that can be expressed in physical violence. This is underpinned by the game that men play with each other, of who can be the scariest and therefore retains the rank of the alpha male within any group.

As I embarked on the development of a shamanic practice, I was then led to deal with fears that were far less specific and reached deep into my psyche. I classify this as existential fear. Fear in respect of the negative aspects of spirit, and the negative power that they can express.

I have seen this work in reverse though, several times, when the powerful negative presence of a spirit affirms a person's belief in spirit per se. And with the right attitude of seeking to learn from these experiences it is possible to become stronger and more courageous. It is also through this engagement with the shamanic path that I have caught myself in the trap of certain egoic actions, throwing into sharp relief how these actions can be unconsciously running and lead us in the wrong direction.

For me the last and perhaps the hardest place to deal with fear has being in my intimate relationships, to be able to speak from my heart and be exposed and vulnerable has been the greatest challenge. When we are traumatised our fear-based responses are closer to the surface, and our fear reaction can be activated far more easily. When we move towards fear the speed at which we can process our emotions increases. When we are in a positive and resourceful state we are in a place of infinite choice. If we are living in fear our choices are diminished, we tend to be in reaction, rather than being able to respond. Trauma states are the complete diminishment of choice, as we look daily even hourly searching for the triggers to our states. We become reliant on the chemical release, the emotions associated with the trauma. It is like entering a house and declaring 'There is a hoover somewhere in here, I know it' and franticly emptying all the cupboards until it is found and then in a demonstration of explosive emotion declaring that you knew all along there was one there. Please forgive the ludicrous image as it is a serious situation of emotional contraction that we can be subject to. What I am trying to illustrate is that the fixation on the trigger is a self-fulfilling prophecy.

The warrior seeks to be in the place of infinite choice or to return to the place of infinite choice as soon as possible, especially in the face of aggression. The warrior has a duty to maintain their level of awareness in order to create harmony. This is where the training leads, the tempering of body, mind, heart and eventually spirit. It is as if mastering fear gives us the key to work with all other emotions. Our attitude begins to welcome the arrival of fear, with curiosity to know where it has come from, and we're excited by the prospect that going towards it will make it vanish. The warrior then finds that developing this relationship with all the so called negative emotions starts to integrate them. The emotional states do not like this move towards them, they are used to being pushed away (which just makes them stronger) and therefore it establishes a win/win strategy. If you take fear as your greatest teacher you are putting your-self squarely on the path of the warrior.

There seems to be a sequence of ways in which we relate to emotions: Starting with a complete lack of choice and almost an addiction to the chemistry that the traumatised states release in us. This locks us in to cycles we can get stuck in, as they are familiar. Here we are in an acutely activated state. Then we have the more normal situation of being caught in habitual unconscious reactions. Through creating more space within us we might move towards a response rather than a reaction. As we become familiar with this way of being, we start to relate more skilfully to our emotions until we become able to act rather than react.

"Between stimulus and response there is a space. In that space is our power to choose our response. In our response lies our growth and our freedom."

Viktor E. Frankl

Emotional state	Relationship to emotion	Internal state	Relationship to space
Acute Activation	Addiction	Trauma	Lack of choice
Unconscious Habit	Reaction	Stress	Normal
Conscious Choice	Response	Calm	Spacious
Skilful Action	Action	Equanimity	Empty

"Tenderness contains an element of sadness, as we have discussed. It is not the sadness of feeling sorry for yourself or feeling deprived, but it is a natural situation of fullness. You feel so full and rich, as if you were about to shed a tears. Your eyes are full of tears, and the moment you blink, the tears will spill out of your eyes and roll down your cheeks. In order to be a good warrior, one has to feel this sad and tender heart."

Chogyam Trungpa 'Shambala' P58-59

Many years ago I was in a photographic shop in Cambridge, this was before the advent of digital cameras. It was a time when film was used and we took our films to be developed and often had to wait days to collect them. As I browsed around the shop, I noticed a Buddhist monk called Mr Ato enter. I recognised him because I had sat in meditation with him previously. He had assumed an almost regal presence while conducting the meditation session and I had been inspired by his powerful presence. He was a contemporary of Chogyam Trungpa's and had fled Tibet, after he had gone out for a walk from his monastery and on his return it had been destroyed.

I observed what was taking place in the shop, there was some problem with Mr Ato's photographs. The clerk behind the counter seemed to be implying that it was Mr Ato's fault. The clerk was quite angry and from his demeanour it appeared to me that he may well have made a mistake and was blaming it on Mr Ato. Mr Ato commenced to apologise wholeheartedly "I'm so sorry" he repeated again and again bowing at the same time, with such gentleness and humility. He did not do it once he did it many times, until the situation began to change.

When I reflect upon it now the interpretation of his apology seems more to be saying "I am so sorry that you are suffering," He continued to apologise for several minutes, until the clerk softened and began to accept responsibility for the mistake that he had made. By the time this was complete the clerk was smiling and laughing with Mr Ato, saying he would have it fixed in the next half an hour, and the atmosphere that was left behind when he exited was one of relief and delight. This episode has stayed in my mind for years, it was a powerful experience to witness this skilful humility. He was apologising for the pain the person was in, he was taking nothing personally just creating space for the situation to change back to something more joyful.

I have more recently had the opportunity to engage in this practice, apologising for many situations where others were holding things against me, feelings of anger etc and in a wholehearted attempt to relieve them of this unnecessary suffering I have apologised. Within the Buddhist tradition this is called rolling all blames in to one.

CHILDLIKE QUALITIES

The qualities of the child are often overlooked, yet they are essential to long life and happiness. They are natural states we tend to leave behind in our quest to grow up yet may even be essential to the discovery of our true nature. If we can find the connection between the childlike qualities and the attitude of the warrior we become open to the capacity of the playful softness of the child tempering the warrior's discipline. We even encounter areas where the innate childlike quality may be more advantageous to us than the warrior's attitude. So we seek to cultivate intentional states that we encounter as children, thus recognising their importance and validating them. While seeking to integrate and develop them in order to harness their important characteristics.

The child is essentially unconditioned, free from prejudice, free from taking things for granted, we could even say in a pure state. Children are relentlessly present, play full, brimming with energy and display great emotional flexibility. They're imagination is their greatest tool, they take nothing too seriously and prefer to play continuously. Their innocence can delight us, and their continuous curiosity can infuriate us. They are still in touch with a simplicity of perception, that paradoxically cannot easily be fooled, yet they are often in the state of complete wonder at the unexplainable mystery of it all.

In a world where children want to grow up quickly, lose their innocence, and value is placed on worldliness and knowledge. It is no wonder that the qualities of the child are not considered important for us as adults. We must also acknowledge that no one gets through childhood unscathed. And it is possible for the disillusionment and trauma that we can be exposed to being replayed late on into adulthood.

In education we value the logical mind and its development to the exclusion of the imagination. One of our most preeminent scientists Einstein said:

"If you want your children to be intelligent read them lots of fairy stories, if you want them to be really intelligent read them more fairy stories".

What Einstein means he qualifies in another statement:

"Logic will get you from A to B imagination will take you everywhere else".

In the science of shamanism chapter, I explore in Einstein's own words the imaginative methods he used to make his great breakthroughs.

The skills of nature awareness, skills perfected by the Apache scouts, to be able to move through nature creating no disturbance, are skills that are innate in young children. I've sat and watched my children play outside, with the birds singing in the trees directly above them. This is not something that occurs for most adults and I have had to engage in a great deal of training and practice to be able to accomplish this for myself as an adult.

Imagine if we reared our children in a way that values imagination, curiosity and wonder. There are educational systems that seek to produce whole human beings as opposed to brains on legs or worse still, cogs in the machine.

IN THE PRESENT

BEGINNERS MIND

"In Japan we have the phrase *shoshin,* which means "beginner's mind." The goal of practice is always to keep our beginner's mind. ………If your mind is empty, it is always ready for anything, it is open to everything. In the beginner's mind there are many possibilities, but in the expert's mind there are few. "
Shunryu Suzuki, *Zen Mind, Beginner's Mind:*

The first quality that we are going to look at is children's ability to remain in the present. This is a quality that we can lose through being preoccupied or actively try to eradicate by creating a sense of knowing.

We know how everything is going to play out, or how it went last time or we are projecting some new idea of how it will be that is good or bad, and this idea is in between us and the experience. Or our head is filled with thoughts. This distances us from the present and what might unfold as we engage with what is happening. The concept of beginners mind is similar to Mindfulness. Though I do prefer the term empty mind over mindful. (I would characterize it more as heartful with empty mind).

Within Zen we find the concept of beginners mind. Beginners mind is about remaining in the present, in order to clearly and fully experience whatever is taking place. Firstly the mind needs to be empty in order to receive or perceive something new, and then in order to continue learning we need to approach what we are practising as if we are engaging for the first time. We find that children are already in this position. As adults we have to re-learn beginners mind. In fact to return to beginners mind we find it is unlearning that is required, and when we understand this principle we find our learning and development can grow exponentially. Unlearning or "not doing" as Castaneda calls it in Journey to Ixtlan, draws us away from focusing on the goal and helps us rest in the process. How present we are in the process is what determines our capacity to learn and connect directly with what is. The journey becomes the goal.

Castaneda talks about "stopping the world" i.e. dropping our description of the world for a direct experience of it. Letting go of our self-construct in order to purely experience, what he calls "seeing"

"The internal dialogue is what grounds people in the daily world. The world is such and such or so and so, only because we talk to ourselves about it being such and such and so and so. The passageway into the world of shamans opens up after the warrior has learned to shut off his inner dialogue." Carlos Castaneda

It is the unsolicited dialogue, we are wanting to stem the flow of and in the chapter on stalking oneness we look at how the practice of stalking has the capacity to "Stop the world" in this way.

As a martial artist we can practice movements thousands of times, if we practice them unconsciously we do not grow in our practice. If each time we enter the practice session, the dojo, we come with a beginners mind our capacity to learn and grow is exponentially increased. The idea that we know something can block us from gaining further insight about it. We fall into a rut and perform the same actions mindlessly. Any way that breaks us out of our ruts keeps us in a greater state of awareness and helps to keep us more present. We need to attain the rank of experienced beginner rather than expert.

"In the highest level a man has the look of knowing nothing ."
Tsunetomo Yamamoto, Hagakure: The Book of the Samurai

It is the same with the skills of survival, and bow drill is a prime example. If we pay attention to every mistake we make and can understand what caused the mistake, then we become more skilled at fire making. When we have made every mistake possible, we will be able to make fire every time without fail. If we continue to bring this beginners mind to bear we never stop learning. This is very similar to the principle of investing in loss. We are paying attention to our failure in order to transform it into learning.

A student once came to an eminent teacher asking to train with the teacher. The student wanted to demonstrate how committed he was and he said if the teacher accepted him he would train every day. The teacher rejected his request, so the student said he would train day and night. Still the teacher rejected the student. The student said he would train at every moment. The teacher still rejected him. Finally the student asked why the teacher rejected him. The teacher replied if one eye is always on the goal there is only one eye to see the way.

"Treat every moment as your last. It is not preparation for something else."
Shunryu Suzuki, Zen Mind, Beginner's Mind: Informal Talks on Zen Meditation and Practice

CURIOSITY

In order to remain in the moment we need to maintain a level of curiosity a level of inquiry into what is happening around and inside us.

Contrary to the old saying "Curiosity killed the cat" it is curiosity that keeps the cat honed and very much alive.

When we recognize our propensity to rest in assumptions and how this can deaden our experience, we need something to keep us awake and engaged. Something to break us out of our rut. Children are consumed with curiosity which tends to be shut down as adults and the real challenge is how we reignite this vital quality. If we are able to reengage our curiosity, perhaps through remembering to ask questions we encounter a continuous dialogue with the universe. Tracking is the pursuit of asking questions that draw us ever closer to the multiple mysteries that are around us. This practice awakens our awareness and increases our engagement with our experience. Sherlock Holmes, though a fictional character, embodies the use of curiosity and tracking, paying attention to miniscule details, continuously running experiments and honing his senses. We can use these skills to solve the mysteries of life.

Another avenue that can generate a lot of energy is being inspired to learn. We can become hungry for knowledge and information. Children are curious about everything and when we are inspired to learn, we discover a tremendous drive to find out, which brings a lot of extra energy. All of the subjects that I am most interested in, could be continuously studied until the end of ones days and it would be impossible to know all there is to know about them. This can at first seem really daunting, realising the vast range of knowledge and skills we may want or need to practice and discover. The vastness of the mystery and the expanse of things we do not know stretch before us blocking our way unless we re-engage our curiosity.

When we begin the study of something that we may never master we are always thrown back on our curiosity, it can remove the dulling nature of boredom from our lives and replaces it with an excitement to face what we don't know with a fresh question.

With the quality of the child we rather take the view that we are immersed in a great mystery and that everything we don't know is an exciting adventure to uncover. If we treat each new area of learning like solving a mystery or engaging with and penetrating into that vast pool of knowledge, we can celebrate each individual part we uncover. Much like a child turning over stones to see what is underneath. Enjoying the sense of adventure that each day might offer as it unfolds some further insight or information. We focus on what we are learning in the moment, rather than on some distant goal of becoming an expert. We are eager to ask the right questions of each day. This type of approach keeps our energy flowing and our curiosity engaged. Rather than feeling overwhelmed at what we don't know.

When as a teacher we are asked a question that we do not know the answer to, we seek to enquire with the student and set about solving the mystery they have presented to us. Or we accept the new homework to be researched later. This attitude allows the teacher to practice with and in front of the students rather than being limited by the assertion that they are an expert and therefore need to know everything. The teacher's is happy to share their failures as well as their successes and therefore continue to experiment and push the bounds of their understanding.

This became clear to me after I had been teaching for 10 years. I was invited to speak on five live BBC radio several times and each time I was introduced as a survival expert. I found after this appearance on the radio, that for at least six months, I accepted the title of expert. I found this quite awkward as it meant I couldn't fail in front of my students, and therefore could not practice in front of them and continue to learn. I then heard a Yorkshire man talking about experts on the radio. His view, was that an expert, was an 'ex' as in past tense 'spurt' of water. This amusing reorientation help me to let go of the title, and once again feel comfortable to demonstrate, practice and sometimes fail in front of my students, which meant inevitably, that my learning continued. I realised that the title of expert set up a series of expectations that made it difficult for the one with that title to continue to experiment or demonstrate failure in front of their students.

The beauty of curiosity is that it has no end result and so it perpetually draws us into the present.

When applied to our dark and difficult aspects it reveals to us the insubstantiality of those parts we fear are solid and absolute. By exposing them to ourselves we loosen their grip on us and move out of the shadow of shame that they hide under and evaporate in the light of our awareness.

WONDER

"To see the world in a grain of sand and heaven in a wild flower to hold infinity in the palm of your hand and eternity in an hour"

William Blake

Wonder another childlike quality, that is very linked to being in the present moment. It also has the capacity to move us into a place where we see the majestic beauty of some aspect of nature, like a storm, rather than be affected by its chilling torrents of rain and powerful blasts of wind. Wonder can elevate our experience from the mundane and can even transcend extreme physical circumstances. When we wonder at the beauty and majesty in the world around us, rather than tremble at its destructive power. For example if we come across an adder basking in the sun and find ourselves marvelling at its beauty and how rare the encounter is or on the other hand, we run screaming from the scene. It is similar to the mood of the warrior, in that we are choosing our response to be one of moving towards the experience no matter how challenging.

Wonder can transform our experience at unexpected moments. A student once shared a beautiful story of a time when she was very depressed. She had been in a depression for some time and was huddled away from life, while rain poured down outside. As she sat by the window looking out, in the grip of her depression, a ray of light illuminated one raindrop as it rolled down the window. It was then that she realized, in that one drop, there was a rainbow and as this moment of wonder took hold, she realised that each drop of rain that fell contained a rainbow. She recalled, how it was this moment of wonder that had lifted her from her depression.

I was running a survival quest in the Pyrenees a few years ago, one of the groups comprised of three women. They were having trouble deciding on a site for their group shelter. As I did my rounds, I encountered them wanting to use a spot that had the remnants of an old shelter on it. I explained that they were welcome to do this but they had to completely dismantle it and rebuild from scratch. As I stood on the spot and surveyed the giant boulders that were sprinkled over the hill we were on, I noticed one large long bolder that was next to this shelter that formed a cave and looked like it was already naturally half a shelter. By laying branches against this stone an excellent shelter could be constructed in half the time. I pointed to the boulder and asked them if they thought it could be used for a shelter. The response of the two women in the group I was speaking to was "That's what Adel said". Adel had wondered off and as far as I could tell was in a state of complete rapture. Shelter or no shelter it did not seem to matter to her. This was not laziness, she was just so surrendered to the wild mountain top we were on, that she had transcended the need for shelter.

The group went ahead with the construction of the half boulder shelter. I came to see how things were progressing and was impressed by their beautiful shelter. They were involved in a heated discussion about where they should place the fire. Was it better near the entrance, where they wanted to site it, or further back in the shelter. I inspected their shelter and concluded that, the back of the shelter offered a stone wall that was almost a natural chimney, all they needed to do was open a hole in the shelter and the smoke would flow out. When I gave them my opinion I got the same response, "That's what Adel said".

Again Adel had strolled of in a state of wonder. This situation happened several more times over the quest each time Adel had accurately pin pointed the solution and then left the others to come to their own conclusion. Not letting any disagreement interfere with her state of rapture. This demonstrated a degree of wonder that seemed to override the physical and emotional circumstances.

There is an interesting link between wonder and curiosity. When wonder is expressed as a verb it becomes to wonder or to be curious. So curiosity is an aspect of wonder, if we are engaged with what is going on around us then we find more to marvel at.

The presence that curiosity and wonder generate also ties in with an aspect of the fool, in order to be able to find humour we need to be very present. The key is to find novel ways of relating to ordinary things. This creates links that we had not noticed or new interpretations or misinterpretations, that create humorous outcomes. Wonder grows out of seeing things as if for the first time, rather than carrying our preconceptions with us. By resting in the present we can make use of these fresh perceptions to create delight. Wonder comes when we don't take things for granted.

As Castenada suggests the attitude of 'reverend astonishment' brings us into a state of wonder. Yet often our lives are set up with long periods of monotonous activity, looking forward to periods of time off. We get caught in behavioural ruts, that deaden our perceptions and experience. On holiday or when traveling we can more easily get into the flow of magic and wonder as everything is new and different, the skill is to see what is new and different when we are in our mundane normal monotonous reality. We can choose to have an adventure, or have an experience of ordinary wonder.

Changing our perspective can also shake loose aspects of wonder, seeing a vast landscape or sky, or seeing some tiny detail. Slowing down, actually smelling the roses or really being present with a meal or a friend, spending time listening, savouring and appreciating what is taking place.

In order to rediscover wonder there are simple ways that are tried and tested. We take so much for granted so all we have to do is start by removing things that we take for granted. This is why within many spiritual traditions there are practices of fasting and seclusion. After several days of building your own shelter, purifying your water, making fire and finding food, this wonder and gratitude is renewed. You could try simple experiments of removing things from your life that you take for granted and see if it triggers gratitude and wonder.

"Rejoice and see your way to wonder"

Norman Mommens Sculptor and visionary

Appreciation and gratitude are a powerful factor in helping us to get on to the wonder wavelength. Yet gratitude is only going to fulfil its function if it is really felt and meant. This means that being told it is useful does not really help. It is only when we cry out with gratitude from the core of our heart and being that it can become a door way to wonder. Curiosity and gratitude produce wonder, rapture is wonder in action.

One question I love to ask the children on my camps is, would you like to know what it is like to be a tree? Usually they are intrigued and want to know, but are confused as to how someone could show them this. We go into the woods and dig holes for their feet and plant them like trees for at least half an hour. The results are great, even the ones who get up rooted before we get back, realise how the plants and trees are bound to one place and cannot move. They gain a greater respect for the plants and trees. If they stay the course they may realise many deeper lessons. How the trees feel fear at the approach of someone with an axe or the relationship the trees have with the clouds and rain and the stars.

This exercise not only brings insight about the trees, it grounds us and helps us to deeply connect with a particular place. I have used this exercise as a healing for specific ailments as the earth draws out of us heavy or negative energy. If we cannot dig a hole and bury our feet just taking of our shoes and feeling the grass beneath our feet can help. Most martial arts are taught bare foot for this reason.

GROUNDING

Grounding is one of the fundamental principles of warriorship. This is about noticing our connection with the earth continuously. Feeling how our bodies contact the ground and maintaining a conscious connection with how we meet the earth. It is also concerned with remaining in touch with the basics of life, maintaining natural rhythms that help to create equanimity and balance in us.

Aside from slow and relaxed breathing the main physical practice is standing and walking, letting the major muscles release, allowing the weight of the body to be felt and transmitted to the ground, letting the feet be soft. As the muscles relax we can feel the weight of the limbs because the muscles are not so active. The major muscle groups are designed to assist with movement not to hold the body upright, this is the job of the bones and connective tissue. If the structure of the body is aligned correctly, the bodies weight drops to the feet. As the weight arrives at the feet we can feel a sense of lifting coming from the instep and through the inner core of the body. The joints are expanding as they are no longer held in place by the tension in the muscles. So as we relax and allow this grounding to take place we are beginning to stand. We use less energy as we stand this way and we can also imagine a cord dropping down from our centre and connecting us to the centre of the earth. Envisioning this connection can make a profound difference to our grounding. This imagined cord can also lift us up from the crown of the head and paralleling the physical forces we may have started to feel through relaxing the main muscles in the body.

Grounding also means attending to the ground of your life so if you are having a great philosophical discussion and have not done the washing up you are not expressing this quality of grounding. If we intend to practice the skills of the warrior we may be tested to see if we are humbly interested to learn these skills, if not we may find that the lessons in humility come much later. Humility is an aspect of the ground, it keeps us close to the ground then there is not so far to fall. Routine can be used to regain a sense of grounding especially through synchronising with the rhythms of the earth. If we are following natural time, we are more synchronized with the seasons and the land we are living on. Similarly the rhythm of our breath corresponds directly to our emotional state and even the simple technique of breathing in for five seconds and out for five seconds for five minutes three times a day can create emotional equanimity and a state of heart coherence, (see The Heart Math institute).

We need this quality of grounding of rooting to be able to stand our ground. We also need it when we are spinning out and getting disorientated. We need to just stop and regain the connection with the self and the ground. In the internal martial arts we imagine this grounding going into the earth below our feet. Within Tai Chi the main push hands practice is designed to help us test the quality of each-others feeling of rootedness. The skills of survival create a very powerful grounding as we develop the ability to be at home where ever we are on the earth. We also gain a connection and understanding of our back yard, our environment, that means we feel and acknowledge the support it gives us.

Once we have developed the ability to stand our ground all other techniques flow from here. When our stance is correct we accept any force and allow it to flow to the ground and if we make any strike or evasive move we are doing so with the power of our whole body and the power of the earth. This is an aspect that we return to again and again, testing it in various ways in order to establish it as a fundamental principle of all movement and stasis.

I had been training for a number of years on and off and had just immersed myself in a new style for three months. While wandering home with a friend we were attacked in the street by two men. As they went past, the larger one hit my friend Steve and the smaller one hit me twice. When I over-came the shock of the unprovoked and unexpected attack, I looked around and saw the person who had hit me lying in the middle of the road. I had been walking on the outside edge of the pavement and as I was standing reasonably well this youth had fallen over into the road as he hit me. My friend had carried on walking in the direction we were going in and the bigger guy had carried on walking in the opposite direction. Unfortunately he turned to see his mate in the road and my friend who had continued walking turned at the same time, thinking 'Tom 's getting them' I was rooted to the spot and seeing the larger guy coming for me took off, running past my friend at top speed with the large guy on my tail. Looking back, it conjures up a rather comical image with my friend's puzzled expression as I ran past him. The main reason I include this here is just to point out that if you are standing correctly and someone hits you their force can backfire on them.

These skills translate into the emotional realm, as we learn not to take things personally, we can stand our ground more effectively. We can allow emotions to flow through us into the Earth, rather than letting emotions get lodged in our body or egoic self. When we can step into a state of allowing and maintain our energetic integrity, just standing our ground becomes a healing position. We recognize what is our emotion and what emotion is the preoccupation of others.

This leads to the development of our stance (called 'sanchin' in Japanese martial arts) which is how we ground ourselves physically and relates to the choices we make in terms of our actions in the face of the situations we face in our lives. Stance is both Physical and mental and as we enter a survival situation or a wilder experience of nature is crucial. If we recoil in fear and get caught up in complaining about the physical discomfort we may feel, trying to put our wagons in a circle to protect ourselves from the wildness it becomes a struggle for survival. On the other hand we may be energised and delighted to be moving into an expanded realm, unfettered by the stifling demands of our over protective civilised society.

CENTREING

"But if ever the least flicker of satisfaction showed in my face the master turned on me with unwonted fierceness. 'What are you thinking of?' he would cry. 'You know already that you should not grieve over bad shots; learn now not to rejoice over the good ones. You must free yourself from the buffetings of pleasure and pain, and learn to rise above them in easy equanimity, to rejoice as though not you but another had shot well. This too, you must practice unceasingly---you cannot conceive how important it is.' "

Zen and the art of archery p85

Centering has both a physical and an emotional basis. The spot just below the belly button is the physical centre of the body. Within the softer arts it is critical that the body moves around this point. If this point moves the whole body moves. From an emotional/mental perspective, if we are drawn away from keeping our attention in the present by our emotions or thoughts then we are out of our centre.

Our first task is to be aware of how our physical mind is continuously striving to create conflict with itself. It is as if we have many different parts of ourselves that are all clamouring against each other. The critic, the judge, the well behaved child, the adventurous self, the parent, the rebel, etc... We may experience this as the passing of unsolicited thoughts through our mind, we have a beautiful thought and we rise with it or we have a despicable thought and we are dragged down by it. Yet these thoughts and the voices of the different parts, are just passing through our mind and only when we have some leverage on them can we begin let go of identifying with them. It is our identification with them that makes us feel good or bad about ourselves and how we create inner conflict. If we decide not to believe a single thought then we can help to shut down this seemingly ceaseless action of the mind. Naming them as thoughts and watching them float past can give us leverage and create space between the thought and us. Also developing the Alpha brainwave state can quieten the physical mind, allowing a level of adsorption and flow that encourages the cessation of unsolicited thoughts. The self-story telling we engage in can become a form of self-harm. As well as meditation there are various forms of movement that can help to slow down and even eventually stop the physical mind from this process.

Part of this process is how we look at thoughts and emotions and how they work together to remove us from the present. For example, our partner is away from us, and we begin to wonder if they are being faithful or not. This is a thought and might trigger a cascade of emotion and further thoughts and ideas about the actions of our partner. Or we might have a vague feeling that we then attach a story to, building on this foundation with our thoughts. This snowball effect of thought and emotion is happening all the time and only when there is enough space in us can we even notice it, in order to undo the process. Realising that when we next meet with them we will be able to sense if our story has any truth in it or we can check out whatever thoughts or feelings we were experiencing, by asking them directly. When we returned to our centre, by remaining in the present, our mind and emotions do not stray and create a story that ninety nine percent of the time has nothing to do with reality.

Fear can knock us out of our centre, we can even be removed from our centre by being overly happy. We need to find the place of balance within our emotions, able to feel them and let them flow through us, without them getting stuck. If we can feel the emotion without the story attached to it, it can flow through us more swiftly returning us to a state where we can interpret reality more accurately.

When our physical mind is filled with unsolicited thoughts it is hard for us to remain present. The key to the cessation of thought is in not believing a single one of them. If we observe our thoughts and emotions, we discover they like to stick together, either a thought will have an emotion attached to it or the other way round. We have grown so familiar with, and used to the internal dialogue that the concept of not believing our thoughts is perhaps a little bit scary. Once we realise that it is not a dialogue but a *monologue*, perhaps we can see how the continuous argument we create in ourselves is merely the mind in conflict with itself. When we can return to a 'zero position' emotionally and mentally we can be fully present and choose what takes place.

I was packing up from an outdoor event and the last day had been a torrential down poor. This continued on through the day it took us to pack down. I had been set up in the woods, and once fully packed up, with my trailer hitched on to the back of my four by four tried to drive out of the woods. I had road tires on so I needed to create more traction to drive out. I was slowly cutting brush and laying it down to edge my way out, which was working perfectly. One of the site crew came over and asked me to wait till a site vehicle came over to tow everyone out. I knew I could slowly edge my way out without damaging the ground, so carried on. Not long after another site crew member came over shouting and swearing at me to stop. I suggested that as he had lots of energy, perhaps he could push the trailer as I tried to drive out. He continued his barrage of insults which provoked a Ki-ai using a word I cannot repeat here. A Ki-Ai is a spirit shout, once I had made the Ki-ai I was back to a normal state of infinite choice. This shout had put this rather large man in to a trauma state: fight. He confronted me and began to remove his jacket, in the obligatory pre fight build up. I stood calmly, intending only to yield. It was muddy, the ground was uneven and covered in brash, but I had a good spot to stand on. I was grounded and after the shout, fully centred again. As I looked him in the eye, I could see that the red mist had come down, there was no turning back for him. He had already lost, as far as I was concerned. A small circle formed as some of the other site crew members turned up, having heard the fracas. My partner then stepped in courageously and appealed to each of the other site crew, in turn to hold back their man. Each one in turn looked at the floor. I had had to adjust my footing as she had interposed, and her entreaties then turned to me 'Just move the car, and this will be over'. I thought about it and decided that fighting was a waste of time, someone would most probably get hurt and having choice I decided to move the car. I then pulled the small axe out that was tucked in to my belt at the back, as I could not sit down with it still there. I had been using it to cut the brash, and got in to the car. Pull out the axe, was like a red flag to a bull, as the member of the site crew who had been poised for a fight started up 'I'll bury that axe in your skull etc..' I moved the car and then the vehicle arrived to tow us out. As I organized this the enraged guy followed around behind me mimicking how he was going to attack me. I ignored him, so he turned his attention on my partner. This completely freaked her out and she left the wood leaving her car behind. Once I and the trailer were out, I found her, calmed her down and then went back to retrieve her car. The upset site crew member was there directing operations, insistent that my partners car would come out last. I realized that he was still traumatised and had no choice. So I decided to demonstrate how we can have choice. I went over to him and apologized for shouting at him. This had been the only thing I had done. He immediately gave the instruction for my partners car to be towed out next. A month or so later I met with the event organiser, who asked me if I had heard about the mad axe man of the woods. This made me laugh, as I explained it must have been me and told him the whole story.

Chogyam Trungpa in 'Meditation in action' describes a simple and skilful means of creating space between us and our thoughts. When they occur in meditation, he suggests we label them as thought and then watch them pass like a cloud in the empty sky. If we can create a tiny bit of space between us and the thought, then there is the possibility of no thought. When we are experiencing a lot of unsolicited thought, it is an indication that our mind is predominantly in a Beta state. As in the chapter stalking oneness, the use of wide angle vision assist us in entering an Alpha state, thus swiftly and simply reducing the amount of unsolicited thought that tends to take place in our mind. Initially we can experience this during our practice of stalking, and after a time, this becomes a more permanent state

OVERCOMING OBSTACLES

We will always encounter obstacles whatever we are doing. The issue is how we relate to the obstacle. When we see the obstacle as a problem we will increase our suffering. The obstacle might even create pain for us, but if we relate to it skilfully it may not create suffering. There is a clear distinction between pain and suffering. Pain comes from some kind of event, suffering is what our mind and emotions do with this event. Obstacles can be physical, emotional, mental even spiritual.

However, when our attitude is one of 'whatever the obstacle is, is the next thing to deal with'. Then we start to create a different relationship with the obstacle. When we attempt a task generally our assumption is that it will be straight forward. We need to do something and this is how it's done and we leave no space for mistakes and miscalculations or unforeseen circumstances. When we are mindful i.e. paying attention in the present, centred with little distracting thought or emotion, we find that if we encounter so-called problems, we take them in our stride.

When our attitude is tempered by looking at obstacles as part of what needs to be done, we immediately remove the suffering that they cause. We have not bargained on that obstacle being there but there it is, it is part of what is, therefore we need to relate to it directly. The tendency is to relate to it indirectly and for it to cause ongoing problems for us.

One of my mentors a close family friend, martial arts instructor and shaman helped me to understand this many years ago. I was staying with him and his two sons and my brother. It was Pancake Day and we had no eggs. Dan suggested we jog to the shop which was a mile away to get some. I had just given up smoking and taking up running and a mile or two seemed like a good distance from a gentle jog.

We all set off and about half a mile along the road we came to a turning. Dan said, 'Oh you haven't seen the fairy stones, would you like to see the fairy stones?' I said 'Yes that sounds interesting' At which point, Dan's youngest son, Callum said 'Oh no, not the fairy stones'. Dan suggested that Callum could jog the half mile back to the house and wait for us if he did not want to come. Instead Callum decided to come with us, I thought Callum is only nine, we can't go very far or very fast. How wrong I was, seven miles later we found ourselves on the wrong side of the river Esk to the shop. We decided we would do a river crossing, so we bundled our clothes up onto our heads and wandered the riverbank looking for a good place to cross. It began to snow as we surveyed the wide fast flowing river, that at certain points forms the border between England and Scotland. I noticed a place where stones slowed the water creating a funnel in the middle. that was quite fast flowing. I chose this as our crossing point, Dan, Calum and I swam across holding our clothes on our heads. My brother Ben and Dan's oldest son Avashi continued to search for a crossing point. I could see hikers in the distance making their way along the footpath that ran along the side of the river they were on. Our scene would make an unexpected and amusing sight for the Walkers perhaps. Dan swam back across to encourage them and they all swam together to the far side. While I shook my hands and stamped my feet to get the feeling back in to them. Much refreshed, we continued the last several miles to the shop, bought some eggs and returned with a pretty good appetite for pancakes. I have still to this day never seen the fairy stones.

It was many years later when I was in the Amazon, with a group of students, my brother leading our expedition into the jungle near Iquitos. When this training came into its own. My brother had told me and one of my companions, eager to reach our encampment at the end of a ten kilometer hike into the jungle, 'When you have gone over 22 hummocks (small hills) you will reach the camp'. Both Dave and I had counted 22 of these hummocks, we were walking in temperatures and humidity that was similar to being in a steam room. I had insisted on carrying my own pack, my colleague had given his over to one of the locals we were travelling with. My friend sat down exasperated at the fact that we clearly were not at our endpoint. I could see we had not arrived and we could sit here and wait or continue and find our destination. I sat for a while to rest and then explained that we needed to continue, to be fixated on the fact that we had counted 22 hammocks would not get us there. So eventually we continued another few kilometers and 15 or so more hummocks further into the jungle we eventually arrived at a beautiful hut on stilts next to a sinuous stream which was obviously our destination.

This type of mentoring I have encountered in different ways through various relatives and family friends. It helps me to feel held within an indigenous tradition when I think of these times and the effect they have had on me. I know that every time I go to visit Dan some type of 'shopping trip' like the pancake expedition is inevitable, some strenuous adventure, that will pull me out of myself, expand my energy and connect me with the landscape and Dan.

I have also sought to bring my children up with this type of activity. The last adventure of this kind we went on was on Dartmoor several years ago. I had all three of my youths with me, I had previously taken two of them when they were children to camp out in the middle of Dartmoor at my favorite spot, Lucky tour, just with bivi bags much to the surprise of the two other campers we met there. My youths wanted to revisit the spot. So we started up the river, I suspected the spot was a mile or two up river, it turned out to be around four. As we approached each bend I remember saying 'it must be round the next corner'. We found a cache of oyster mushrooms on the way and I asked the universe to have a fire going by the time we arrived. As we the tor came in to view, smoke rose from the valley floor. A group of climbers were busy scaling the rock faces there. One of their number hated climbing but liked hanging out with his friends, so had started a fire. We cooked the mushrooms offering him som,e which he refused. By this time it was getting dark and the four mile route along the river had been quite treacherous, and navigating it in the dark was not going to be easy. So my older son suggested we find an alternative route back. The return route by road is about eight miles, so I was delighted to return this way. We stopped for chips in a pub on the route. What was most heartwarming about the 'shopping trip' was that at no point did any of them complain.

ENERGY

The next aspect that is required to understand about oneself is how to generate and build energy. The warrior has abundant energy similar to that of the child. There are many practices that strengthen and clear the energy channels in the body to allow more energy to flow. Simply expending energy by running or exercising tends to change our state releasing endorphins and uplifting us emotionally and helps to build our energy to be able to deal with what life throws at us. We can release stress and build physical endurance and become more at home in our bodies.

Richard Branson when asked what do you do to increase your productivity? responded "go to the gym".

As we develop an awareness of energy and how it works we become able to do more than we previously thought possible.

Play is the key here, if you observe a child at play, they have what seems an infinite amount of energy and appetite to play almost to the exasperation of the adults looking after them. As adults we can get dislocated from this ability this vitality. One aspect that always delights me is the way this can be reactivated in the adults I work with. While playing stalking games, where they are given the opportunity to play a very sophisticated game of hide and seek, with the tools and knowledge that as children we would have loved to have. I see this quality remerging, when we are engaged with our own excitement, which helps us access our energy. I also recognise how making fire seems to unleash a great deal of energy, as well as regaining self-esteem.

The engagement with something real, like wild fire, can really increase our energy. Plunging into freezing cold water or being out in nature, perhaps an encounter with a small bird or some awesome creature in the wild. These experiences touch us at a fundamental level unlocking our energy and excitement making our energy more available to us in our everyday lives. From the warriors point of view a physical practice that engages us with continued learning develops our energy.

It is imperative for us to find strategies that build our energy, one of the key aspects of martial arts is to do this. As this affects our attitude in a positive way, we develop practices that help us meet our resistance and move through it. Once we have developed a measure of energy we then have to develop the capacity to contain and direct it in a useful way. Containing our energy interestingly, tends to be more to do with what we don't do, than what we do. We often engage in habits that diminish our energy, causing energy to leak away, and more often than not if we let go of these habits we can contain far more energy.

Once we are feeling energised we then have the capacity to direct that energy. Within KI Aikido the concept of extending KI is one of the fundamentals. If we are extending our energy, it empowers our actions and we find more support. It is our mind that moves our energy in this instance, so where we put our intent, determines where the energy flows and influences the outcome.

MAKING A GESTURE

I had a friend when I lived in Bristol who would always come round in a very depressed state. I liked this friend but found after he left I would be left carrying his depression, having often taken up hours of my time to be present for him. So I decided to make a gesture with him. I came up with what I considered to be a win-win strategy for us both.

The next time he came to my door I said 'Ah, Steve I'm just going for a run, would you like to join me?'. The first time this happened he declined and left, I went back to the kitchen table sat down and continued to drink my tea. The second time he came to the door perhaps a week later I said, 'Ah what a coincidence, Steve I'm just about to go for a run, would you like to join me?'. 'I don't have any running shoes on' he said. I suggested we could jog to his house where he could pick up some running shoes and we could go from there. So we set off, once he had his shoes on we began jogging. This took at least an hour and a half and his house was only five minutes away. As we moved to the outskirts of Bristol towards open country we encountered an area strewn with litter. I could not pass it by without doing something about it and began to pick the litter up finding a large bag and beginning to fill the black bag with litter. My friend who was an environmental activist, was both shocked and delighted to discover that it was possible to make a small difference to the environment whilst on a jog. We filled a large black bag with rubbish and found a bin to deposit it in and continued on our way. Once we got back his mood was buoyant and cheerful we shared a cup of tea and I went home.

The third time he came to my door I said 'Hey Steve I'm going for a run do want to come?' He replied' yea sure'. So off we went with the same outcome as before. The next time he came to my door he was no longer depressed he seemed cheerful, energised and full of life and I invited him in for a cup of tea.

I had made a gesture with my friend, without criticising or saying anything, I had just shown him how to change his emotional state and to build some energy. I was able to do this because my mentor and shamanic friend Dan had made a gesture with me, many years before, when I was at a very low ebb in my life.

Sometimes when I have mundane tasks to accomplish, I will bounce between engaging in practices that I enjoy, in order to build enough energy to be able to skip through the mundane tasks. Engaging in things we love to do builds energy and though we may not be able to spend all of our time transforming our work into play or working at things that we are passionate about. We may find a small amount of time spent engaged in something we love, gives us the energy to accomplish the mundane. Another strategy is to view the mundane task as a meditation, in this way we integrate mind and body, performing our task with full presence. This can also be done by practising our grounding skills while waiting in a queue, or some principle of movement that we are working with, when we are sweeping the floor etc.

"The true science of martial arts means practicing them in such a way that they will be useful at any time, and to teach them in such a way that they will be useful in all things."

Mymoto Musashi The book of five rings

My favourite example of this is in the films the karate kid; where the young boy is trained in martial arts through performing DIY tasks for his teacher. His teacher Mr Miagi gives him clear instructions as to how to perform each task. Within each task, like waxing a car, sanding the floor and painting the fence Mr Miagi has embedded a different defensive technique. The task provides the necessary vehicle for much repetition of the movement and the quick embedding of the technique in the young student's body.

YEILDING IN ORDER TO ADVANCE

The warrior's only opponent is her or himself. The ultimate act of warriorship is to reach out with the heart. To seek to be open hearted in any situation, to see through aggression and meet the pain that inevitably lies beneath it, firstly in oneself and then in others. To actually stop and feel your own pain, with compassion, is what is required. To feel your own sadness and grief gives the space for the tenderness to grow in you. As you soften towards yourself, melting your judgement, your criticism of yourself your tender heart grows. As we become able to feel the pain without the story our emotions remain fluid.

This provides the opportunity for the warrior to act rather than react. One becomes more flexible. It is the genuine embodiment of compassion. As it brings softness where there is pain and can transform rage to grief. The image used by Trungpa is the meekness of the Tiger. That the softness and relaxed attitude is coming from a place of power, not a place of weakness and at the core of this power is softness in the heart, a listening heart.

We are moving towards a state where there is nothing to protect, no territory that we do not want others to step on. With nothing to protect there is immediately 50% less aggression in any situation.

It is the quality of awareness of the warrior that we need, to be able to get over ourselves. We need to watch our own mind as if it were our opponent in battle and in the same way strive to meet it, to know it. So we can take the next step.

The quality of awareness that the warrior cultivates comes from purposefully putting the self in a situation where if you don't pay attention you will get whacked i.e. in the dojo. This is a pure state as it brings you fully into the moment. This state is sometimes called mind fullness. Yet it is as much defined by the emptiness of the mind as by the level of absorption in what is being done.

It is some form of ongoing practice that gets us out of our mind, or calms the unsolicited thought. We move from thought to experience through the vehicle of our practice our discipline.

As our meditation develops we need to move beyond the idea that other people interfere with our state, such and such is happening and it is disturbing my meditation. We need to move beyond the boundary that the peaceful state of mind we develop in solitude, is any different from the resonance of mind we experience when in the middle of the city.

Imagine that an aggressor confronts you; they are threatening you and making some kind of demand. This situation will normally generate feelings of fear and panic. You may feel yourself contracting emotionally. Mentally you may be separating from the person, viewing them as a bad person an embodiment of negativity. At an emotional level they will be feeling this and their sense of rejection and pain that has brought them to the point of threatening you will be answered by your perpetuation of this situation.

Imagine now that you have noticed this person before they have threatened you. You can feel that there is something not quite right. So you extend a sense of attention and brotherhood/sisterhood to this person. A feeling of "Hello, here is another human being who may be in pain." Perhaps they are drunk, and again here we have a choice. Do we attach a value judgement to the fact we can smell alcohol on them or do we consider our own enjoyment of alcohol. Our perspective is shifting from one of dissociation to one of inclusion. What happens when this takes hold when it is a genuine feeling, is that the aggressor is being seen and met so it becomes harder for them to pursue their pain by inflicting it on you. In fact they are receiving something closer to what they might actually need which is the recognition and meeting of another human being. 'What do you need?' is perhaps the best question to be asking them.

These different approaches that are taking place in our mind and heart are to me the highest form of martial art. In the face of adversity to see clearly what is going on, brings it back to a human level of interaction. We are not caught up in our own internal monologue or historical reactions and distracted from what is happening around us, we are relating to things as they are and we are interested in them. Changing our minds changes our reality.

In order to accomplish this we may need some type of training, to give us the accumulation of energy and presence of mind necessary to enter and lead this type of situation. The training could be in martial arts, meditation or some other practice. This process occurs in minor ways every day and we are presented with many opportunities to reassess our choices to act or react. This is yielding in order to advance, we have given up defensiveness, and offer no resistance, we are either meeting with the heart or we might offer a different perspective. i.e." it is not good or bad just interesting."

To express the principle of yielding in order to advance physically, we have to come back to softness and the concept of yielding instead of blocking. Blocking gives information to the attacker both that the attack has failed and the attacker will try something else and information about the body of the blocker. The feeling that we are trying to create is somewhat like when we go to open a door and someone opens it from the other side and we go flying through the space.

We are inviting the attack to come through the space and organising our body around the attack, with the consequence that the attacker will fall on to some part of our body or the floor, in a way that is uncomfortable for them. The other aspect of the yield is that it sets the body up like cocking a gun or squeezing a spring, not necessarily with the energy of the attack, but by responding to the direction and momentum of the attack. Within the physical context this draws us away from technique to principle and developing the feeling of the principle in the body. Rather than practicing technique.

THE WAY OF PEACE

"If your heart is large enough to envelop your adversaries, you can see right through them and avoid their attacks. And once you envelop them, you will be able to guide them along the path indicated to you by heaven and earth."   Morihei Ueshiba

We were walking through a pedestrian precinct in Hove. I was arm in arm with my heartner. Suddenly around twenty young men entered the far end of the precinct, singing football songs. I felt everyone in the street contract in fear. Here were a big gang of rowdy young men, most probably drunk and dangerous. Even the police man that stood in the precinct between us and the young men looked a bit sheepish and scared. My heartner tried to tow me to the side of the walk way to avoid the young men. I had no intention of moving aside, I intended to walk through the middle of them. Internally I was thinking, 'young men singing, how wonderful, I don't get to hear young men singing very often'. We passed the police man and made our way into the throng. The first young man approached in front of the police man and in a pantomime way put his finger in front of his lips and went shhh. At this the whole street burst out laughing. All the young men the police man and all the bystanders. That was the first time I have been in a street that spontaneously erupted into laughter. To me reaching out with the heart and mind, perceiving things clearly is the way of peace.

There are a number of historical figures that are very useful in understanding the notion of martial arts as a way of peace. Moria Ueshiba the founder of Aikido, is one of the more recent Japanese figures, who in 1925 had his first spiritual awakening. After defeating a naval officer's attacks with a wooden sword, whilst unarmed and with no harm coming to his attacker ,Ueshiba went into a nearby garden and had a spiritual awakening that he describes here:

TRUE NATURE

"I felt the universe suddenly quake, and that a golden spirit sprang up from the ground, veiled my body, and changed my body into a golden one. At the same time my body became light. I was able to understand the whispering of the birds, and was clearly aware of the mind of God, the creator of the universe."

From the way of peace Moria Ueshiba

From this and other later experiences, one of which was in 1942 during the Second World War, he developed a vision of the way of peace.

"The Way of the Warrior has been misunderstood. It is not a means to kill and destroy others. Those who seek to compete and better one another are making a terrible mistake. To smash, injure, or destroy is the worst thing a human being can do. The real Way of a Warrior is to prevent such slaughter – it is the Art of Peace, the power of love."

It might seem contradictory to practice an art so that we never have to use it, yet the goal of the way of martial arts is to create peace. Firstly in the practitioner and then in all those he or she meets. Another figure in Japanese history is Mymoto Musashi who attained awakening after many years of extensive training and fighting. In his later years he wrote 'The book of five rings' which is filed with insights. He was born in 1584 and fought sixty duels some against multiple opponents, his first was when he was thirteen.

The last lethal duel Musashi fought was on Ganryu Island, his opponent Sasaki was a very famous swordsman who had developed his own style imitating the flight of a swallow's tail. Musashi arrived intentionally hours late in order to create a strategic advantage.

"The important thing in strategy is to suppress the enemy's useful actions but allow his useless actions"

Mymoto Musashi The book of five rings

Instead of bringing a sword he carved an oar into a bokken (a wooden sword) from the fisherman's boat, that carried him across to the island.

It was during this duel, after killing his opponent he attained satori.

"What I call the void is where nothing exists. It is about things outside man's knowledge. Of course the void does not exist. By knowing what exist, you can know that which does not exist. That is the void."

Mymoto Musashi The book of five rings

Both of these historical examples demonstrate an innate connection between wariorship and awakening, which is similarly the direction that meditative traditions like Buddhism and zen point towards. This ties together the strands of peace making and wariorship and takes it far beyond a situation of holding peace through force or fear.

"All life is a manifestation of the spirit, the manifestation of love. "

Morihei Ueshiba

PLAYFULNESS

"Grown-ups never understand anything for themselves, and it is tiresome for children to be always and forever explaining things to them. "

Saint-Exupéry, The Little Prince

Children are forever playing, and it is their play that forms the basis for how they make their reality. When we play it is as if we have stepped outside of the normal mundane way of looking at things, so our actions have far less consequence. This produces a state of relaxation that creates more flow. Playing is such a primal activity that buried in each of us is a great capacity for it. When we play, winning or losing are not as important as having fun. Enjoyment is the key. We may be very competitive and enjoy competing, but at the end we all know it's just a game.

By bringing a playful attitude to situations where we need to learn we can expedite our learning because we bring the enjoyment of playfulness to the task. Especially when we are developing our training in shamanic skills. A playful attitude combined with the powerful use of imagination can create strong results. Playfulness circumnavigates the physical mind which would otherwise block our journey into the imagination. We may take things very seriously but this doesn't mean that we can't still play. Playfulness takes us into the territory of the Fool, being wise but seeming foolish.

If you observe comedians they are acting in the same way as warriors by yielding in order to advance. They accept the premise and reality of whatever is directed at them, never challenging the statements, they only agree and then transform the statement into something amusing. There is a dance between chaos and possibility. It is only when we are comfortable with ending up looking like a fool that we can be most courageous.

THE FOOL AND THE KING

There was once a king who had a very wise fool. One day the fool upset the King immensely by something he said. The king demanded that he should have is head chopped off for his insolence.

The King's advisers begged the King not to kill the fool, knowing how wise he was and reminded him of the beautiful poetry that he had helped the King write to woo his now Queen. The advisers also reminded him how the fool had averted war with the neighbouring Kingdom, by making such mimicry of the King behind his back, that the neighbouring King could not help himself and laughed so heartily when he was in court, that he decided to sign a peace treaty instead.

So it was that the King decided he would grant a concession: the fool would die, but he could choose the manner of his own death. So the fool was brought before the King and told the gravity of the situation.

The fool with a big beaming smile said 'Ah thank you sire, I choose to die of natural causes'.

"The opposite of play is not seriousness. Play is serious as hell, for it's the most integral learning tool nature has designed."   Floris Koot

The playfulness of children comes with little self-consciousness and therefore they don't have far to fall. The more self-importance we have the more we have to loose. So if we declare ourselves to be a complete fool, then we are already ahead of the game. So cultivating the attitude of complete failure with enough curiosity to help us turn the failure into something of value i.e. laughter, we discover the wisdom of the fool. This might in turn lead us to the sacred nature of the profound shift from forever seeking success to that of accepting our folly. Our normal state is one of avoiding embarrassment and exposure of our wounded self, when we stay in touch with the wound, the difficulty, rather than avoid it, we can find a compassionate warmth and humour that is transformative of our pain and the pain of those around us.

"You think about yourself too much and that gives you a strange fatigue that makes you shut off the world around you and cling to your arguments. A light and amenable disposition is needed in order to withstand the impact and the strangeness of the knowledge I am teaching you. Feeling important makes one heavy, clumsy, and vain. To be a man of knowledge one needs to be light and fluid."

Carlos Casteneda A separate reality

When we use our imagination we are involved in a kind of play. Children's ability to imagine is creative, transformative and easily communicated. Largely as adults we find our imagination gets busy on its own. It invents all kinds of situations and scenarios that might have happened or might happen in the future. Things we can get seriously involved in worrying about. We let our imagination or mind develop the capacity to conflict with itself as we struggle to decide what to believe. Are the good thoughts important? and do they make us worthy? or are the bad thoughts proof that we are a bad person?.

When our mind, thoughts and imagination are unconditioned then we can start to use our imagination as a serious tool for our benefit and the benefit of others. The key to untying the mental knots is rather simple and is based around the idea of belief. Belief is only useful if it is rooted in our own experience. Any belief that is based on something we have been told or on a thought or idea we read is going to set up conflict with in us and between us and our experience. Once these thoughts and ideas become part of our experience then we no longer have to believe them. They have moved into the realm of knowledge. We can recognise if they are the way they have been described or different, because we have run our own experiments, to verify or disprove anything we are told or have read. By not believing any thoughts or anything we are told, we have the opportunity of a much purer, more unconditioned experience of life. An experience of life that is based on what we actually perceive as taking place an experience closer to the perspective of the child.

I have often found myself having to say to students "Try softer" instead of the usual, "Try harder".

It is most often through physical or creative activity that we can re-inhabit, and embody childlike aspects. Whether it is the rolling and break falling of Aikido, the kicking about of a football, or another sport or playing hide and seek with our children. It could also be through some creative act like icing a cake, making a collage or playing music or singing. These activities reconnect us with our vitality. We are brought into the moment to meet the challenge, of skilfully moving or creating.

VULNERABILITY

THE WARRIOR OF THE HEART

THE MEETING OF THE WARRIOR AND THE CHILD

The warrior cultivates open heartedness, a level of vulnerability that comes from a place of strength, from giving up defensiveness. This is an expression of compassionate fearlessness that reaches out to meet our difficulty, inner or outer, and exposes a quality of childlike gentleness, that encourages us to drop our pretense in order to truly meet those around us. Accompanied with tender playfulness, with which we can celebrate the journey, curiosity, keeps us in the present and gratitude keeps us open to possibility and wonder.

"The lover of nature is he whose inward and outward senses are still truly adjusted to each other; who has retained the spirit of infancy even into the era of manhood." ~Ralph Waldo Emerson

How we are in nature teaches us about our attitude as it reflects us back to ourselves. When we remove all the distractions and crutches of the modern world, we discover that we have ourselves to rely on. Our attitude is the first thing that will either enable us to survive or cripple us, even kill us.

Learning how to deal with both, our inner and outer landscape, helps us to become more balanced and engage more fully with whatever we encounter. We need the qualities that are found both in the warrior and the child. The warrior gives us the courage to be open hearted and the power of gentleness. Here the only battle is with the self, overcoming our resistance to being authentically human. Reclaiming the child is a return to an unconditioned state, it allows us to play and imagine freely. This reawakens joy, humour, curiosity, excitement, awe and rapture, which frees up a huge amount of energy and helps us circumnavigate the restrictions of the physical mind.

The attitude of the warrior is based on choices that have been decided beforehand, ways of action or not doing that dismantle the inner constructs that we can mistake for reality. These choices create the right conditions for the qualities of the child to spontaneously emerge.

We arrived at the councilor's house, expecting the same sort of experience as we had had throughout the mediation process. Difficult discussions mediated by councilors who struggled to remain impartial. It was an old council flat, that we entered through a small garden with a small fenced lawn. We had been given such a glowing account of how this retired councilor worked and I certainly was intrigued. She had apparently worked with indigenous elders and was connected to the wolf clan. She had agreed to see us, even though she was retired. We entered her little kitchen and were given cups of builders tea, while Carol, the elder woman who resembling a working class Granma, smoked several cigarettes. We sat round the small Bakelite topped table, Carol declaring that good things happened in the kitchen, so it was an appropriate place to talk.

To this day I do not know what really happened. We sipped PG tips tea from mugs, ate biscuits and Carol asked us a few questions. First she turned her attention on the mother of my two boys and somehow began to dismantle her resistance and anger with skilful questions. I listened and observed until my ex-partner was asked to tell me directly what the problem was. What ensued was a great deal of anger and blaming, directed at me, in a way that cut me to my core, as only those who are close to us can. I reacted badly defending myself and filled with indignation left the table and exited into the garden. I was enraged that again I was being subjected to this stream of what felt like abuse. Eventually after calming down I re-entered the kitchen and Carol turned her attention on me. I do not remember what she did but within a few minutes she had cracked me open and for the first time in my life I felt like I had access to my wounded inner child. It had up till this point been powerfully defended by my warrior self. Afterwards I felt my inner child riding on the shoulders of my warrior self, no longer trapped by past hurts and defense but able to direct the warrior-self. This poem emerged after the session.

Warrior and child

The wise old crone

With fish wife mask

Shakes my centre

Pulls me out

Cracks me open

Breaks through the powerful structure

Of years, bricks and tears

Small frightened

In pain

Unheard

Words blazing all around

I find my child-self crying

Across the years

Defended by the full grown man

The warrior,

Walls of fire surround him….me,

Finding my small self my child part,

Not even I acknowledge his pain

No one ever knew

Today I know, today I feel,

The defences melt into warm tears of relief,

TRUE NATURE

The crone circles my walls of Jericho,

Trumpet in hand

Weeping I feel, I become soft,

I become myself again,

The years of defending left me forgotten,

Not knowing what I was defending,

What value to defend self-pity?

Protecting it hiding it like treasure,

Raw I emerge,

The duel is over and I am dual,

Old and young are again one,

The crone whispers

Only as children will you come unto me.

"Whoever does not receive the kingdom of God like a child shall not enter it."

Luke 18:17

CHAPTER 6

INFRQUENTLY ASKED QUESTIONS AND UNCOMMON KNOWLEDGE

"Have patience with everything that remains unsolved in your heart. Try to love the questions themselves, like locked rooms and like books written in a foreign language. Do not now look for the answers. They cannot now be given to you because you could not live them. It is a question of experiencing everything. At present you need to live the question. Perhaps you will gradually, without even noticing it, find yourself experiencing the answer, some distant day."
Rainer Maria Rilke, Letters to a Young Poet

It took me forty two years to figure out how to question my teachers skillfully, how in fact to be a good student. When I was first introduced to one of my martial arts instructors he showed me through his answers how to ask the right questions in order to be a good student.

My normal protocol was to ask a new martial arts teacher a test question, one that I have asked many times before and have received many different answers to. I went ahead with my test question and received the best answer to date. My question was, "Where is the Qua?", this is the area at the center of the body that generates all the power in martial arts and in many forms of movement. Nathan Menaged's response was " from here (indicating just below the ribs) to here (to the tops of the knees)", meaning all the core muscles were involved in the opening and closing of the Qua. This was the best answer I had had to this simple question so far.

I then proceeded to my second line of questioning, which is to ask a question that is not so much one I want an answer to, but one that shows how much I know. This type of question is not really an enquiry but merely a question to put myself on a par with the teacher. I don't recall the precise question, It was along the lines of offering a metaphor for the exercises we were engaged in. Nathan's response was along the lines of 'Let me practice with that idea for a year or so and I will get back to you'. I soon realised that this type of question was a waste of my time, the other student's time and my teacher's valuable time.

I then gave up all such questions and began merely to ask, 'Nathan I don't understand what you've just explained, could you explain it in a different way again please?'. With this question I exposed myself amongst my class mates, appearing to be stupid, showing my lack of understanding and ignorance. This took some courage as I was training with many other skilled martial artists of different disciplines. I had to be okay with this perception because the result of this was that Nathan would find another description, one that then allowed me to understand what he was trying to teach me.

On that particular day I learnt between ten and fifteen martial arts principles, principles of movement that are universal, that can be applied to everything. In my previous 25 years of training I had learned three principles. (Admittedly one of which kept me safe when caught up in a gang fight situation). So to learn fifteen principles in a day made me light up like a light bulb and so did my teacher because he could see that some of his life's work was being transmitted to one of his students. I was filled with energy and understanding from that day keen to research all of the new work I had been shown, It has taken many years of practice for these principles to sink into my body.

During the class each time I asked 'Nathan I don't understand what you mean can you explain it again?', I felt throughout the room the other students thinking, 'thank goodness somebody has asked him to explain it again, I did not get it either'. Because they were struggling in the same way that I was. Why is it that we will create a culture of shame around asking questions in a class. It took some courage to appear stupid for a moment to then be wise for the rest of my life. This is a strategy that is really required for us to learn not just from human teachers but also from the earth and spirit.

'I don't understand this?', 'Show me what I need to know right now?', this type of question helps us to move forward in our lives. 'Show me the next step?' These are the type of questions that we should be asking not the overarching question of philosophers. What we need are questions that help us to see what is right in front of us, how we forge ahead with a clear compass for our life's direction.

At the end of that particular day of training Nathan came and thanked me for asking him so many questions. He said that every time I asked him to explain a principle again, it made him a better teacher, because it forced him to find another way to explain the principle, he was therefore honing his capacity to explain the principles. At the time I did not understand why he thanked me and I had not really understood what had taken place. It took me several months to understand that he had shown me how to be a good student.

There are also very much the wrong kinds of questions similar to my second question, questions that are self-aggrandising or are missing the point. One of the other students kept trying to ask questions. Each time he began Nathan would say, 'You no questions' ,which I thought was extremely rude. This fellow student never managed to get a question out during the class, so I had no way of knowing the type of question he would have asked. Years later I learned the nature of his questions, which were somewhat missing the point of the style we were practicing.

It was not until a few years later that I had a student like this, whose questions wasted every ones time. The questions were from his overactive mind, that merely bred more similar questions, that brought him no closer to any real answers. It seemed to be a way of drawing attention to himself, rather than looking at what he really needed to know. It also took up a great deal of every one's time. And so I found myself saying to this student 'You no questions'. I suspect that the other students thought that this action was very rude of me. I was merely saving a lot of time on what was a short weekend course.

It was two months after the course that I received a letter from this young man thanking me for the action I had taken with him in the class, as he had begun to understand what he was doing and the benefit for his understanding of himself..

If we can use the approach of asking what it is we need to know right now, when we are confronted by a wise teacher, then we have the capacity to expand our understanding greatly. If on the other hand we are caught up in egoic questions then we will not get anywhere.

QUESTIONS IN THE REAL WORLD

Science is first taught as a series of facts to memorise where as the key to being a skillful scientist is really being able to ask the right questions, to challenge the assumptions that are passed down with in the field of what we are taught as fact.

"The scientist is not a person who gives the right answers, he's one who asks the right questions."   Claude Lévi-Strauss

It is not just in science that the capacity to question draws people on to great discoveries it is also within the arts. It is through questioning the old forms that modern art has emerged. Artists like Duchamp were central in breaking down the perceived barriers between art and life. Jackson Pollock and Rothko questioned the materials they were using. Through the questioning of conventions something new has been created something fresh and of our time.

"Great drama is great questions or it is nothing but technique. I could not imagine a theatre worth my time that did not want to change the world."   Arthur Miller

Explorers have also been questioners, wanderers, wondering what lies beyond the limits of their horizons. They were Inspired to following strange tales to distant lands and new shores on quests of discovery. Our incessant questioning has driven us to even send a man to the moon.

"Judge a man by his questions rather than by his answers."
Voltaire

It is this process that has helps athletes become the best, finding unconventional answers to problems that have long held them and their competitors back. It is really in moving beyond convention that we find answers to the questions that we seek, bringing something new to light. We could rename the great thinkers as the great questioners and this would help us to understand what is taking place in their minds.

"Socrates himself said, 'One thing only I know, and this is that I know nothing.'
Remember this statement, because it is an admission that is rare, even among philosophers. Moreover, it can be so dangerous to say in public that it can cost you your life. The most subversive people are those who ask questions. Giving answers is not nearly as threatening. Any one question can be more explosive than a thousand answers."
Jostein Gaarder, Sophie's World

A QUESTION OF TRACKING

When asked what the single most important thing that Tom Brown Jr's mentor Stalking wolf taught him, he answered 'The sacred question', he then went on to say that what was most important was to ask it at least fifty times a day. On previous occasions he also said that when Grandfather used the word 'sacred ' it meant that what he referred to had a deep significance and that in itself would require more inquiry. The sacred question is the foundation of tracking and the engine of awareness. It drives our awareness to uncover mystery after mystery. To put tracking in a nutshell Tom Brown Jr offers an approach which consists of the three sacred questions and these three questions addressed three very different levels of experience.

The first question is 'What happened here?', this question draws us to a very clear physical understanding of the movements involved in the animal or person's track and from this we can discover the ABC of reading that movement in the track. As we break the track down into its different parts and see each part being affected by different aspects of movement, to the point where we can read accurately direction, speed, head position and many other factors. For example whether the animals belly is full or empty, any injuries it might have, shivering and farting, tiny movements that it would be hard to see with the naked eye if we were watching the animal.

I have asked this question sometimes up to fifty times of a single track and it is possible to almost see the animal there in front of you as the information starts to stack up.

We can also delve deeper and ask the second sacred question 'What is this telling me?' and as we ask this question we start to be drawn into the relationship that the track has with everything around it' why the track was made, where the animal was going, how it was travelling. We start to get a glimpse into the emotional content; was the animal in a normal gait, was the animal hurrying, was it taking its time, was it moving too slowly, was it injured, was its bellyful therefore it was moving away from its feeding area, perhaps towards a cool sheltering spot. As an example these are some of the things that we begin to extrapolate. We also start to see the relationship between the track and the sounds of the birds that are still going on around us, aware of the forests alarm system, that the animal we are tracking would also be paying attention to. With our focus on the track we start to be able to detect a whole web that the track both affects and is affected by, we are no longer just working with the physical, we are unravelling the energetic connections between all things.

At this point we might ask the third sacred question 'What does this mean?, this draws us into a deeper level of the symbolic significance of what we are tracking. If we study the meaning of different animals and their significance in a symbolic context we always find that the symbolic meaning derives from specific physical characteristics that the animal in question exhibits and it is the expression of those physical characteristics that form the animal's symbolic meaning. This is expressed more fully in the chapter 'Conversations with Nature'. The question 'What does this mean?', brings our attention to the significance of what is going on in our lives at the present moment. Understanding and putting to use these three questions, we become both trackers of the earth and trackers of ourselves.

It was no coincidence that in the writings of Carlos Castaneda he was tutored in tracking and stalking. Tracking and the questions involved in tracking offer an engine of awareness they drive our awareness to understand the mysteries that we encounter, as Tom Brown Jr says 'Awareness is the doorway to spirit '

THE SPIRITUAL SURVIVAL ADVANTAGE

As we delve into the field of survival and bushcraft we are seeking to widen our knowledge and understanding. The skills are extremely practical and yet we either may be motivated by other than practical goals or we may discover that as our knowledge grows we are drawn deeper into the layers that we find.

The samurai are a good example here or the martial arts in general. When we follow this path we are looking for a method that really yields results. We want to be able to defend ourselves, develop our confidence and become fit and healthy. Throughout the process we test each other's presence with sparing or push hands to see how well we are integrating these skills. We become aware that as we progress that the level of physical power needed diminishes, as our skill level increases, and perhaps we discover that at a physical level our greatest power is the power to yield.

We can discover the power of our minds and encounter aspects beyond the physical that are also in play. The level of our awareness, our experience and competence with understanding energy and our own emotions all begin to move us into subtler levels of combat and defence. We may even get to the point of being able to discern the spirit of our opponent and may develop our own fighting spirit as part of our training. All of these aspects add to the greater understanding of the specific subject we are studying. If we are learning universal principles, then they will flow out into all the things we do and the relationships we make. For us to deny that our work does not take us into the sphere of spirit is only to admit that we have fallen short in our study of our chosen subject.

This may be a strong statement, yet we already acknowledge the importance of psychology with in sport, the psyching out of an opponent even in the arena of chess playing, is a major factor where the battle that is going on is purely in the mind. Our own mental strength can also push us far beyond the endurance of our body. When we are in "the zone" we have reached a point of synchronicity of mind and body that lifts us to another level. Yet when we talk about spirit, we all too easily can confuse it with religion. I am talking about a practical philosophy or spirituality, born of experience. An approach that fosters through repeatable processes either a state or resonance that allows results to emerge that then build our belief our knowledge.

Meditation for example creates a vehicle for us to enter different resonances, effectively moving through the shackles of the physical, mental and emotional experience, thus allowing us a greater freedom and purity.

What we tap into is a sensitivity that goes beyond the normal levels of perception. Even with in the levels of physical awareness we can be considered to be psychic when we detect things beyond most people's normal range. Yet we are just operating at a level of observation and attention, that's survival advantage is no longer considered relevant by society, because we have sought to make everyday life easier for ourselves.

Hence setting up systems and external authorities that determine things as trivial as the weather forecast or as important as our health, while our capacity to know where to find what we need to live in the environment has dropped away. This has taken away our need to be keen observers, clear instruments of perception, as we have created so many external ways to accomplish the tasks that sensitivity had been used for over generations. This has also diminished our experience as human beings and is the cause of a great deal of disconnection and stress in society. When we reconnect with the earth we find that these sensitivities are required, to be able to identify plants in all seasons, to read tracks left where there is no clear print, to listen to the voices of the birds, to make fire in the old way and to determine the weather patterns.

Yet when we want to be responsible for our own survival, we are seeking to engage as many levels as possible, to maximise our chances while minimise the energy we need to expend.

There are two questions that I devised to see what the proverbial 'person in the street's' view of spirituality was. The first I asked was: "You are facing a duel to the death and you have a choice of fighting someone who has trained only physically, or someone who has trained physically and spiritually, which opponent would you rather fight?"

Ninety percent of people responded that they would rather fight the one who had only trained physically. There were a few anomalies i.e. people who said they would rather fight the spiritual warrior as they were likely to have mercy and not kill them.

I realised after a while that this was a very male orientated question and devised a second: "If you were on your death bed and could be attended by a medical doctor who was just trained in allopathic (western) medicine, or one who was also trained in spirit healing and other (so called) alternative medicine as well as being a medical doctor which would you choose?"

The response to this was a hundred percent, choosing the doctor trained in a spiritual way as well. No one I asked just wanted the regular doctor. What this illustrates is that in a life and death situation we would rather rely on a subtler levels of connection, which we call spirit, than just on the physical. This shows our unconscious orientation towards there being a great deal beyond the physical.

Would you rather follow a guide to reconnect you to nature who just has a physical understanding or one who also has a deep spiritual connection?

QUESTS

The universe seeks to answer any questions that we ask. In the Bible it says 'seek and you shall find, ask and it shall be given'. Ask the universe a question and it shall be answered.

All scientific research is based on the asking of questions, if we find a good question that there is not yet an adequate answer to, we have found a quest. It is questions and quests that drive our lives. If we are content not to ask any questions and to be satisfied with the answers that we find around us, our lives will never uncover any mystery or discover anything beyond the half-truths and accepted wisdom of the people and culture around us. If on the other hand we find that we are driven by questions and we find a particularly good question to follow, our whole lives can then become the most wonderful unfoldment of that question. The story of Buddha is a great example, as he was driven by a question, he gave up being a king to find the answer to how to move beyond suffering.

Questioning is an art and creating a question is a skill full business. Because the question we create is the one that will be answered, this is the reason the question why is not a particularly productive one to ask. One teacher of mine once said 'Why is not a shamanic question'.

Forming a question is somewhat like making a primitive arrow. It involves the skill flint knapping of an arrow head a skill that requires over a hundred hours to learn, in order to create a satisfactory result each time. This skill is we could equate with the skill to reduce the question to a precise point. The next job is to find a shaft that is straight and true, many look that way until they have been cut and then the bends and kinks must be taken out of them with patience. Then feathers for fletchings are needed to keep the flight of the arrow level and on target. To attach them we need to make glue and fine cordage and to put them carefully in their place. Next we carve a notch to fit the string of the bow, making sure the whole arrow holds together as one. The creation of a question is somewhat similar, in that we are putting together components that need to be straight and true to the point and balanced. So that once fired into the unknown it will hit its target. If our question is unwieldy and hastily put together we will end up either with an answer we don't understand or dislodging many more questions that seek to hone our original question.

Choygyam Trungpa in his book Shambhala, in the chapter celebrating the journey talks about the bow and arrow of action and intellect, or of tenderness and sharpness and how through inquisitiveness we can find out about the reality of our world through questioning . He talks about the process of asking questions and how they are inexhaustibly answered by the capacity of the universe to communicate with us about the questions we ask.

"The sense of trust is that, when you apply your inquisitiveness, when you look into a situation, you know you will get a definite response. If you take steps to accomplish something, that action will have a result- either failure or success. When you shoot your arrow, either it will hit the target or it will miss. Trust is knowing there will be a message.

When you trust in those messages, the reflections of the phenomenal world, the world becomes to seem like a bank, or reservoir of richness. You feel that you are living in a rich world one that never runs out of messages. A problem arises only when you try to manipulate a situation to your advantage or ignore it. "

Shambhala Choygyam Trungpa Page 69

The universe seeks to answer these questions, the bow that we use is a clear mind and a passionate heart then once fired the answers will return to us in some form, often in unexpected ways: a chance meeting, an overheard conversation, unconsciously picking up a book and flicking through it, or being overcome by a strong feeling, being reminded of an amusing story, there are many ways in which these questions are answered. Our trust and openness is required, once we have asked the question, that the universe will find an answer and a clear way to communicate it to us. This is questioning at a spiritual level and the questions that we have may well be practical questions as much as spiritual ones. What we might become aware of, at some point in this process, is how fashioning a question is similar to making a prayer.

'Be careful what you wish for as it will often come true' Oscar Wilde

This is true of both prayers and questions and even thoughts if we go along with the Buddhist view of mind speech action. It is a great field of experimentation and one were some experiments produce better results than others.

If we break the word question down into: Quest-I-on we see that a good question is really a quest.

As we move along this quest we often find that experimentation and research is required. We try to bring to life a question by testing it out seeing if the principle or the tool we have been shown works and how. For me there is always some questioning or research running every day. This puts the search in to our research.

One aspect of the spiritual path that sits alongside meditation is that of inquiry. Inquiry employs the use of questioning, to question the beliefs we hold, and the very nature of the inquirer.

"When the Velcro thoughts and emotions arise, the key is to face and investigate whatever belief structures underlie them. In that moment, inquiry is your spiritual practice. To avoid this practice is to avoid your own awakening. Anything you avoid in life will come back, over and over again, until you're willing to face it—to look deeply into its true nature." Adyashanti, The end of your world.

Questions like 'what is the meaning of life?' are far too broad to bring us any real meaning or enlightenment. We have to hone our questions, in the same way we hone our arrow head, each chip of stone is a greater act of precision. It is what we remove that shapes the question to a single pointed focus. The single pointed focus is required to form the question, yet to receive the answer we need a quality of openness and trust that the universe will respond. Perhaps what we do not realise is that this process has been going on our whole lives and we have not been aware of it. Our lives are shaped by this process. Thought is the primary mover of our reality, then speech and thirdly action. What we dwell upon is what we manifest.

MENTORING QUESTIONS

"Asking the proper question is the central action of transformation- in fairy tales, in analysis, and in individuation. The key question causes germination of consciousness. The properly shaped question always emanates from an essential curiosity about what stands behind. Questions are the keys that cause the secret doors of the psyche to swing open."
Clarissa Pinkola Estés, Women Who Run With the Wolves

Through mentoring, it is possible to see how the act of questioning is what needs to be brought to the attention of the student. That to question is the act that is required, as we transition from being children to young adults. If we harness the curiosity of the child or reawakening it, we can turn our questions into a quest, taking the many uncertainties, concerns and unknowns that we can face as young people into a rite of passage.

With a rite of passage the teenagers are sent off into the wilds on their own to survive and fast for three or four days with the simple instructions to pay attention, to the messages of earth and spirit. To return having asked some questions and possibly with some answer for their lives, some meaning, purpose, direction or understanding, this practice is a profound way to be shown both by nature and spirit where we fit into the grand scheme of life. This has been practised for millennia and I would rather be living in a society where people are driven by their own inner purpose and an understanding of their intimate connection to nature and spirit, however that manifests for them.

This way of working with what are effectively the teenagers in their society, is taking their capacity to question and challenge the authority of the establishment of the elders and creating a context that helps them to recognise their self-responsibility. This is empowering and provides a framework for them to form their own questions and find their own answers. This process also means their lives can be lived from that point forward in communion with all aspects of their world, both physical and spiritual.

"Until modern times, we focused a great deal of the best of our thought upon rituals of return to the human condition. Seeking enlightenment or the Promised Land or the way home, a man would go or be forced to go into the wilderness, measure himself against the Creation, recognize finally his true place within it, and thus be saved both from pride and from despair. Seeing himself as a tiny member of a world he cannot comprehend or master or in any final sense possess, he cannot possibly think of himself as a god. And by the same token, since he shares in, depends upon, and is graced by all of which he is a part, neither can he become a fiend; he cannot descend into the final despair of destructiveness. Returning from the wilderness, he becomes a restorer of order, a preserver. He sees the truth, recognizes his true heir, honors his forebears and his heritage, and gives his blessing to his successors. He embodies the passing of human time, living and dying within the human limits of grief and joy.

Wendell Berry, The Art of the Commonplace: The Agrarian Essays. "The Body and the Earth" p.95

John Young through his 'Art of mentoring', has distilled a method that was used to bring his curiosity to the fore, by his first mentor Tom Brown Jr.

Within Jon Young's approach there are three levels of questioning, the first level asks very simple questions that can easily be answered, the majority of questions that are put to any child or mentee are of this type. Then the mentor starts to ask questions that demand a little research, that demand the mentee to look more deeply at what is around them to see what has been missed. The third level of questioning, revolves around questions that take us perhaps a whole lifetime to answer. These are questions that draw us beyond our comfortable edges, beyond the veils that exist around our minds and in our lives, questions that will drive us to make new discoveries to explore the world around us and our inner world. This approach to questioning is central to the art of mentoring to the way in which it is possible to draw somebody deeply into their relationship with nature. In asking these questions we might well awaken the natural curiosity, that can become insatiable, that needs to be fed with answers and then breeds more questions, that become a doorway to a deeper connection with life.

The next step that this encourages is how we then devise our own questions and with each question we are brought into deeper and deeper layers of research and possibly understanding.

This was naturally the role of the elders, who with only their wisdom as a guide would set about schooling the younger members of the tribe. So when anthropologists and missionaries arrived they could see no school as separate from what was just taking place as a natural process and therefore assumed no education was in progress. Yet ask the right question of an elder and the whole village would stop to listen to the stories and wisdom. Jon Young's experience demonstrates this in a startling way, as after ten years of mentoring from Tom Brown Jr, Tom asked Jon to help him teach at the school he was opening. Jon was confused as this guy Tom, had merely asked him questions for the whole ten years of his mentoring and so it seemed to Jon that Tom knew nothing of nature, as he was continually asking Jon to find things out for him. If we are lucky we encounter mentors who demonstrate these skills to us in a real way.

I was lucky enough to have several mentors like this. One of them was my aunt Ursula Mommens, a venerable potter who taught me to throw pots when I was sixteen. She set me up, gave me instruction and then went off to get on with her other chores .Just as I was about to make a mess of things she would turn up and help. I still have several of the pots I made with her. I realised many years later when I was teaching English woodland crafts, that she had also taught me how to teach crafts.

When I use the term spiritual it would be easy to assume that that was something separate from our physical experience. At a certain level there is no separation, it is more like the fact that the eye can only perceive certain wavelengths from the electromagnetic range, yet we know that there are many other wavelengths such as infrared and ultraviolet that we cannot see. They are still part of the spectrum, but beyond our capacity to perceive. Similarly what goes on energetically and spiritually may be beyond our capacity to perceive, though it doesn't mean that they don't exist. And when we look at brainwave activity we see a correlation between different frequencies occurring in the brain that give us access to perception at different levels. So what we are experiencing are not separate phenomena they are distinct phenomena, phenomena that are occurring at different frequencies.

This process of directly asking nature or spirit relevant questions can reveal a great deal of natural wisdom, helping us to follow our own path. Rather than requiring an intermediary, a teacher or guru. Once the method and process are understood and a real connection is made, the inquirer can learn more directly from spirit and nature than from any human teacher. This makes this path one of direct learning and is unique to the individual inquirer.

The hardest thing to do when asking is to let go of the question, to peacefully rest in the knowledge and trust it will be answered. To surrender the question to the universe.

Reflection is also important, periods of quiet contemplation and meditation, this is a good place to both fire the questions and often helps the answers to emerge, out of the silence and nothingness they come bringing their illumination. Each time the process is fresh and different with the questions answered in the most unexpected ways.

It is our curiosity and inquisitiveness that is reawakened bringing the energy of the child back into play.

"How many hours are there in a mile? Is yellow square or round? Probably half the questions we ask-half our great theological and metaphysical problems-are like that."
C.S. Lewis

The beauty of curiosity is how it brings us right into the now and has no end point. We come to realise it is not the answers that are important, often the answers stop us really getting to know anything. We learn the name of a plant or bird and then we have killed the mystery, we think we know it because we can name it. While questions keep us engaged stop us taking anything for granted.

"The Wilderness holds answers to more questions than we have yet learned to ask."

Nancy Wynne Newhall

CHAPTER 7

SACRED AND WILD

RITES OF PASSAGE

"They are the sons and daughters of Life's longing for itself. They come through you but not from you, and though they are with you yet they belong not to you."

Kahlil Gibran

The young boys are called by the elders to meet by the central tree, in the middle of the village. The mothers wail and cry, some cannot let go of their sons, the elders have to hold the mothers back and restrain them. The mother's grief fills the air, a tearing to the bone, a terrifying fierceness, at the loss of their boys, their children, their babies.

The elders make a break for it with the bewildered youths following. The youths are unsure of the next step, confused at their role in the tribe. Their growth into self-consciousness, no longer allows them to feel safe in the gender fluidity of childhood, of moving between the women's and men's camps. Wanting guidance from the elders, to be shown how to be strong in the world, respected by their peers and yet able to express the same patience and love their fathers showed them. The youths yearn to feel worthy, to find their gift their power, to live up to the promise of life and the stories they have been told round the fire, late into the night under the vastness of stars. They know how the earth supports their lives, as everything is gathered or fashioned from the land on which they live. They have heard stories of how spirit speaks to the worthy, guiding them with beautiful and subtle clues, helping them to understand the intricate relationships between humans and their many non-human brothers and sisters; leading the hunters to the deer, steering the tribe away from danger or the simple daily communications of gratitude with the ancestors, earth, water, fire and air.

The elders lead the youths deep into what they now experience as wilderness, to return them home to the bosom of mother Earth, so that where ever they set foot on their return will be their home. The youths, are now eager, curious, excited and terrified in equal measure. The youths are seeking the next step for themselves, they have no grief of the loss of their childhood only the promise of a life lived with connection to the vastness of life. An understanding not just of the workings of nature and survival, but also of their inner landscape of its depth and mystery.

They are brought to the elder's fire, held in a circle and taught the mysteries of life, nature, spirit and the heart. They would be taught through stories, laughter, communion, ceremony, powerful searching questions and life threatening challenges. In the time before time, it would have taken many moons to be made ready to complete the final challenge, to Quest, to start to ask their question of life.

The youths would have sat alone far from their known lands, exposed to the elements, fasting, seeking guidance from the great mystery, the source. They had to push past tiredness, past hunger and thirst, through boredom, past the stations of irritation, annoyance and anger, into vulnerability. Suffering strange incomprehensible dreams, speaking in tongues, speaking in silence, and then at last crying deep from within, from the broken heart of the forsaken, calling for true guidance, for a life to be lived with purpose. And only then finally finding total surrender and letting go. No expectation, just gratitude for the release, for the opportunity to pray. And from that allowing of the not knowing, something stirs, a subtle voice, a feeling, a murmur, from the strangely silent land. The whisper of the ancestors calls them to attention, to pay attention. The sudden appearance of the stag through the mist, the eagle's eerie cry or the dewdrop on the spider's web illuminated by the rising sun. They unexpectedly stumble upon their grander self. Beyond whom they thought themselves to be. Like a giant gong being struck deep within them.

Now remembered, born back to Earth mother and Spirit father, no longer just the child of their birth parents but a child of mystery, a child of the universe. Through their humility, their letting go, they have shown their worthiness to see a vision of becoming, of finding their gift, their passion, revealed as a path to becoming truly Human.

The youths return weak in body, but with their spirit shining. Tenderly they carry the treasure of their search, their quest, though not yet able to see their gift, and so they tell the story of their journey to the elder's. Wide eyed and with tears running down their wrinkled cheeks the elders hear the tales. Nodding and reflecting back the beauty, the courage the gift and the young men begin to see themselves reflected in the elders eyes, in the elders hearts.

The young men are brought back to the village, and the whole village comes to welcome, to receive, to celebrate the hearful, young men. The mothers weep for their sons safe return, they can no longer call them children, or their babies, the mothers and fathers have felt the grief the loss and have accepted that now they are expected to support the new status of the fledgling adults.

In the act of questing is the possibility of understanding the process of gaining wisdom from life's experiences, that carried through a life brings one to the door of eldehood. There is a difference between growing old and growing wise and it is inherent in this type of natural contemplation.

The emergent quality of youth ,the rebellion, the requirement to go their own way, can be supported by the elders as the youths are taught to rely on their own guidance. To navigate through life with the inner compass of connection to nature and spirit.

WRONGS OF PASSAGE

GANG FIGHT

"Something in the adolescent male wants risk, courts danger, goes out to the edge – even to the edge of death."
Robert Bly, Iron John: A Book About Men

I was returning from a night out, with a few pints of larger in me. It was cold and I pulled my leather jacket tightly around my neck as I walked home. My hair was cropped short as I had been training for my brown belt. A young man approached me, "You look like a hard bastard, can you help me??!!" he said. As a martial artist, I felt like I was a member of 'the moral up liftment society', so I asked what the problem was. The young man explained that he and his friend had got into a taxi to go home and realised they did not have enough money to pay for the taxi. So they asked to be brought to a cash point, to get some cash out and instead were driven round the back of the buildings we were in front of and thrown out of the taxi and beaten up by a gang of youths.

I agreed to help him look for his friend, as the young man I was talking too had run off and was worried that his friend could be in a critical condition. We walked around the block looking for his friend and found no sign of him. We got back to where we had first met, on the corner of Jamaica Street, and there across the road was the taxi. It was parked in front of a newsagent with all the shutters down, except for the front door. In the door way were the youths who had attacked this young man.

He marched straight across the street and confronted the youth in charge, who at my estimate was the oldest at around eighteen. Bold I thought, but stupid, and somewhat unwillingly I crossed the street to back him up. As I came on to the pavement space between the taxi and the open door way, the gang surrounded us. Using one of the few principles I had learned from my kung Fu training, I held up my hands in a non-threatening way saying "Let's just all stay calm". The principle relies on the understanding that maintaining a proper distance from a possible attacker, means that nine times out of ten, it is possible to defend an attack, while if they are allowed within range, nine times out of ten they can strike before they can be defended against.

The young man asked, "What have you done with my mate?", and the response he received was, "We put him in the f*****g B.R.I.(Bristol Royal Infirmary) and we are going to put you there to if you don't f*** off ". Moments after this a foot flicked out of the door way and caught the young man under the chin. He stumbled back passed where I stood, seeing an opportunity, another of the youths stepped in and punched the young man. By this point the young man was passed the end of the taxi and into the road. Another youth pulled out a bike chain and wacked the young man around the ribs, at this point he ran off. He was alive, perhaps a fractured jaw, a cracked rib, but alive I thought.

I was left standing amongst these youths, I looked at them, they were thirteen to sixteen years old, they were children, they were not young men. They were acting like a pack of dogs. Even the eighteen year old was acting out of pain. They had no other way of earning peer respect or finding their place in the tribe, their only road was violence.

I assessed the situation, I stood amongst five of these youths. A chain had been pulled out, the next step in the escalation of the situation was that a knife could be pulled. I was confined by the taxi and a lamp post so no spinning techniques were possible, the best way I thought of dealing with several of them at once. Yet I had maintained my space the whole time and even though I stood amongst them none of them had found a way to attack. They were youths, no they were children, I thought, how could I possibly attack a group of children. I decided to walk away, to try to show that fighting was unnecessary. That one could be in the midst of this type of aggression and leave with a powerful dignity. I began to walk away with full attention, if anyone had tried anything, I would have had no mercy. And I think they felt the powerful meekness that I chose to express. The leader called out "leave him alone" as I walked off.

I left with a profound feeling of sadness, no adrenalin response, just deep sadness, that these young men, these boys had no other way to express themselves. The sadness came from recognition that as there was no rite of passage for them, they had created a wrong of passage. They had the sense of community, the camaraderie, the hierarchy, yet they were steering themselves down a path without heart. One of creating terror and fear rather than dealing with their own grief, their pain, then inflicted on others, the continuation of the trauma they were feeling. This type of misunderstanding of the transition from youth to adult is prevalent, in the hazing that goes on in sports teams, university fraternities and many other situations. Ignoring this turning point turns this powerful life rite into a pale reflection at best and a dangerous sanctioning of psychotic behaviour at worst. We currently live in a society of uninitiated men and it creates a very unsafe and dangerous society. It becomes a society of adolescents, rather than one where men are tempered and have the courage to be in the soft power of their hearts.

EXPLORING THE INNER LANDSCAPE OF SELF-ESTEEM

"In ordinary life, a mentor can guide a young man through various disciplines, helping to bring him out of boyhood into manhood; and that in turn is associated not with body building, but with building and emotional body capable of containing more than one sort of ecstasy." Robert Bly, Iron John: A Book About Men

Six thousand five hundred men under the age of forty, take their own lives each year in England. There are many contributing factors to this. Men are taught that expressing emotion is not manly, that men are not as sensitive as women. That as members of the patriarchy men are responsible for the horrors wrought by millennia of patriarchal oppression. With gender issues becoming so fluid our youths are finding it increasingly difficult to find their place within the social structure and understand what their role might be. Having elders to offer guidance, with perspectives that build self-esteem and engagement with life is now more needed than ever. Our youths also need to explore and understand the emotional and spiritual dimensions as they enter adult hood. They are separated from themselves, from nature and their inner world. Perhaps they are offered religion, which turns out to be more of a history lesson than an experience of the divine. So they look at drugs as a way of exploring their consciousness.

In many Earth based cultures there is skilful holding around the psychotropic substances that grow on their lands. They relate to these as sacred teaching plants or medicine and provide ceremonial holding to those seeking to learn through this process. This helps those who wish to try these approaches to remain safe and not suffer unnecessary psychological damage. As can happen when experimenting with recreational drugs. This route is not necessary if the power of the imagination is intact, as there are other experiential routes to understanding our inner landscape that do not use these medicines. Some of the practices that can yield comparable results are meditation, shamanic journeying, sweat lodge, guided visualization, rites of passage and dreaming. When working with the medicine, a level of inner stability is required. As it can be a rocky road, amplifying inner states and presenting experiences that appear real like when in a dream. It is intention that forms our rudder here and much like the quest or question, we form a precise intent to steer us towards some understanding. Like the questioning we also need the capacity to surrender, to let go of the intent or question for it to be answered. How safe we are is dependent on the skill of those holding the space and our own inner stability.

The drug taking that many of the youth engage in, I think is an attempt to understand the inner states that can be experience, to feel ecstasy and to create freedom from conditioning or oppressive emotional experiences. As our society offers few other outlets for this type of exploration.

There are several profound shifts that take place when we undergo a rite of passage. For the person undergoing the rite of passage, though it might hold fear and apprehension, it is the next step in their development so it feels like the right direction to be moving in. The rite of passage holds the possibility of revealing our gift to us. This is our power, our offering to the world, what we perhaps do not realise is that our gift is not for us, it is for those we give it to. To be able to offer something, to have something to give, is both our power and strongly bound up with the self-esteem of a man. Men's sense of value often comes from their gift, their purpose, their passion. This is also true of women, yet there are other aspects that seem to have higher value for women, such as their close relationships and how they are held and perceived in their community, not to say that these connections are not shared by men as well. Though there is a primacy of identification with the role around their work, that can create self-esteem in men.

Men's self-esteem also comes from their sense of connection. This connection has many components: to self, family, lovers, friends, community, nature and spirit. I would suggest that this aspect is of even more importance to our young women. Yet as I have stated both of these characteristics are required for self-esteem in our young people and can be enhanced through rites of passage.

Another aspect that is hidden within the rite of passage and I have not found mentioned in western culture in any form, is how the transition to a young adult is far more painful for the parent than the youth. It requires a great deal of discipline from the parent to be able to let go of the child aspect of their sons and daughters. If this is released at the rite of passage and the parent is capable of forging a new relationship with their young woman or man then the young person is released from the parental holding, that otherwise will remain until the parent dies and only then will the son or daughter feel the release of that holding. So this is part of the gift we can offer our children, is to release them to become more themselves. This does not stop us from still being there to offer them whatever support they might need. But we are moving towards recognising them as equals. This is another step on the ladder of self-esteem for the young adult.

TRANSFORMING DIFFICULTY

INTO LIFE LESSONS

During the holding of many camps and ceremonies there are often beautiful and complex situations that emerge. By relating to them skillfully, they weave us deeper into the magic of what is possible offering ways of transforming how we work with the people around us.

Around ten years ago I was running a rite of passage camp for a group of young people. Amongst the group was the son of a friend, who was a few years older than those who were there for the rites of passage. As an older teen, he held sway over several members of the group and through the initial stages of the preparation, took a standoffish attitude to the proceedings. This meant that three of the teens who had come for the rites of passage, were ambivalent about their participation. They were swayed by the older teen, his attitudes and thoughts. The group was being pulled in one direction and then the other. It was not until he found his place within the proceedings, that all the teens decided to go through the process.

We were preparing the sweat lodge and I asked if he could help me sort out the wood for the fire. His reaction was more positive that I had expected and during the fire wood collection, I realised that his stage of life needed honouring too. His enthusiasm showed that he wanted to be included in some way. I asked him if he would be the fire keeper for the sweat lodge and he immediately agreed. It was at this point that all the vacillation of the other teens stopped. By accepting the role of fire keeper, a role that supported the process for the younger teens, while giving him a sense of responsibility and respect the others all got on board.

While working with those in a camp setting we may be able to cultivate the space and skillful attitude to be able to transform difficult circumstances into powerful life lessons. This may or may not be possible for us in the normal run of our lives. Yet it is here that it is often needed as much, if not more, than with those we might be working with. It is in these circumstances that we are really tested and that we can create lasting bonds and in the process do a real service for our young people.

EACH DIFFICULT BEHAVIOUR

COMMUNICATES A NEED

A number of years ago my oldest son asked me if I would buy him a game on his X-box. I agreed and gave him my credit card details. I was not using my credit card much at the time, so checked my credit card bills about seven months later. Only to discover that twelve hundred pounds had been spent by him on my credit card. When I discovered the amount I was furious and am glad he was not present to witness my response. Once I had calmed down, I began to question what it was he was asking of me by this act. I realized, he was firstly saying that he did not understand the value of money. Secondly, I felt he was asking to be mentored into how to come into the world of work. So when I confronted him with the discovery of his spending spree, I explained that I realised he had done it on purpose, that it was not a simple mistake. That he could either pay me back, by working and paying me, or he could work for me and work off the debt. I said I would pay him half the wages he would have earned working for me. I was running several festivals a year at the time, so I asked him to help with this and of all the festival helpers I had he was the most reliable and consistently helpful.

At one event that my son was helping at, we had some helpers on site, including a single mum and her rather disruptive son. I had to leave site to get various supplies and on my return found my son on the job I had left him doing, not only was he doing the job but also mentoring the younger disruptive boy into helping. It was after this that the disruptive lad no longer caused any trouble. I realized at this point that my strategy was working, seeing my son mentoring this disruptive lad. He was passing on what had been passed to him.

Three years later he had paid it off and we have developed a great working relationship. At the last festival I ran in Devon one of the greatest pleasures of the whole event, was putting it up and taking it down with my two sons.

Had I just got angry with him, not only would I have damaged our relationship nothing would have been accomplished. By trying to understand what he was telling me, through his actions, we were able to move through a complex and difficult situation positively, creating many opportunities for us to spend time together.

COMMUNICATING WITH THE IMAGINATION

When we talk to children if we remember that their imagination is in full flow and they are playing the whole time. Then getting them to do what we ask and having a great deal of fun is possible at the same time.

A mother was trying to put sun screen on her seven year old son in front of my pitch at an outdoor event, I was recently teaching at, his squirming was making it impossible to put the sun screen on and his mother was getting more and more frustrated. At last I could not hold back and went over and challenged her son. "I bet you can't be as still as a statue for two minutes". With this he froze and his mother almost in shock was able to finish the job with ease.

This is just one simple example of how we can communicate and make our life easier and theirs more fun. I also witnessed a situation on a camp site many years ago, where one boy was being bullied by some of the other children. After a little while the boy drew his imaginary sword and challenged the bullies to a duel. It was fantastic to see this young boy defend himself with his imagination, the other boys of course joined in the mock battle and he became the instigator for their games from then on.

SACRED AND WILD

"The Wild Man doesn't come to full life through being "natural," going with the flow, smoking weed, reading nothing, and being generally groovy. Ecstasy amounts to living within reach of the high voltage of the golden gifts. The ecstasy comes after thought, after discipline imposed on ourselves, after grief."
Robert Bly, Iron John: A Book About Men

In his book Iron John, Robert Bly talks about the wild man trapped in all men. How the key to the wild man's cage rests under the mothers pillow and how he has to steal it to free this part of him-self. The mother is acting as the custodian for the son's wild masculine self. Somewhat like the rite of passage, where the mother recognises that she is losing the capacity to control the young male, as he becomes empowered, he might even become dangerous

The rite of passage delivers this key to the man, granting him a powerful freedom. It is only freedom however if the young man is brought into connection with Earth and Heaven, as his new broader parents. Within his connection to the Earth, is his capacity to feel at home where ever he stands on the Earth. Here in rests his connection to his vitality, grounding and sanity. The connection to Heaven, is his capacity to commune with spirit and those aspects beyond the physical, awakening in him a keen animal like sensitivity to energy, feeling and insight.

It is also useful for the young man to experience the dignity of the compassionate heart of mature men, so he understands what is required to grow into his Sacred Masculine. His physical power needs to be balanced by how he inhabits his own heart. The sacred masculine holds the understanding that all is love; that suffering and negative action is only caused by the absence of love. One approach to repair this crucial factor, is how we love ourselves, or how we pay attention to the love that flows through us.

There is an anecdote attributed to Albert Einstein, that expresses the notion of absence of love leading to negative consequences quite skillfully. Whether it was actually Einstein or not is a matter of debate.

The professor of a university challenged his students with this question. "Did God create everything that exists?" A student answered bravely, "Yes, he did".

The professor then asked, "If God created everything, then he created evil. Since evil exists (as noticed by our own actions), so God is evil. The student couldn't respond to that statement causing the professor to conclude that he had "proved" that "belief in God" was a fairy tale, and therefore worthless.

Another student raised his hand and asked the professor, "May I pose a question? " "Of course" answered the professor.

The young student stood up and asked : "Professor does Cold exists?"

The professor answered, "What kind of question is that? ...Of course the cold exists... haven't you ever been cold?"

The young student answered, "In fact sir, Cold does not exist. According to the laws of Physics, what we consider cold, in fact is the absence of heat. Anything is able to be studied as long as it transmits energy (heat). Absolute Zero is the total absence of heat, but cold does not exist. What we have done is create a term to describe how we feel if we don't have body heat or we are not hot."

"And, does Dark exist?", he continued. The professor answered "Of course". This time the student responded, "Again you're wrong, Sir. Darkness does not exist either. Darkness is in fact simply the absence of light. Light can be studied, darkness cannot. Darkness cannot be broken down. A simple ray of light tears the darkness and illuminates the surface where the light beam finishes. Dark is a term that we humans have created to describe what happens when there's lack of light."

Finally, the student asked the professor, "Sir, does evil exist?" The professor replied, "Of course it exists, as I mentioned at the beginning, we see violations, crimes and violence anywhere in the world, and those things are evil."

The student responded, "Sir, Evil does not exist. Just as in the previous cases, Evil is a term which man has created to describe the result of the absence of God's presence in the hearts of man."

After this, the professor bowed down his head, and didn't answer back.

The young man's name was Albert Einstein.

WILD WOMAN

"Be wild; that is how to clear the river. The river does not flow in polluted, we manage that. The river does not dry up, we block it. If we want to allow it its freedom, we have to allow our ideational lives to be let loose, to stream, letting anything come, initially censoring nothing. That is creative life. It is made up of divine paradox. "
  Clarissa Pinkola Estés, Women Who Run With the Wolves.

Many of the elements in the passage above relate not just to men, but to women and at the risk of mansplaining and with multiple apologies for even daring to set word in this direction, here goes.

The rite of passage brings full embodiment to the young woman, connection with wild nature in a way that brings recognition of her interconnection with all things, in a visceral and bodily way. Having the power of creation and birth like the great mother, able to participate fully in this sacred ceremony of creating and bringing forth life. Helping her to feel embraced, invited, held by the village, amongst the community of women, in the wider society and the universe.

This rite of passage to the wild self may happen naturally or through many routes. In these days of rites of passage being ignored, we find that women either find elders to mentor them or work together to bring themselves through these thresholds. Yet life always offers these opportunities and sometimes we awaken, as we are squeezed through the cracks in our lives.

"The doors to the world of the wild Self are few but precious. If you have a deep scar, that is a door, if you have an old, old story, that is a door. If you love the sky and the water so much you almost cannot bear it, that is a door. If you yearn for a deeper life, a full life, a sane life, that is a door."
 Clarissa Pinkola Estés, Women Who Run With the Wolves.

Then there is the connection with intuition and spirit, that when it rests at the centre of her being brings out the power of the warrior in her, making her unable to do anything against herself. Listening deeply to herself in everything, she becomes able to learn from the difficulties of life and to even go beyond the story.

If a woman or a man is to become a mentor, a warrior, then they have to choose to learn from life and the rite of passage can be the first time this process is introduced to the youth. This can lead to developing a clear relationship to what is considered the dark aspect, to treat it with as much respect as the light. To recognise that as life breaks us down, it clears away our reliance on the story of the self. This grinding away, untethers us from the perception of safety, that the small self tries to tempt us with. In doing so it smashes our dreams that are based on what we have been told and clears the way for the vastness that is beyond imagining. So the rite of passage prepares us for these later life stages and the young people in turn benefit from being held by those who have taken this journey.

"There is a time in our lives, usually in mid-life, when a woman has to make a decision - possibly the most important psychic decision of her future life - and that is, whether to be bitter or not. Women often come to this in their late thirties or early forties. They are at the point where they are full up to their ears with everything and they've "had it" and "the last straw has broken the camel's back" and they're "pissed off and pooped out." Their dreams of their twenties may be lying in a crumple. There may be broken hearts, broken marriages, broken promises."
 Clarissa Pinkola Estés, Women Who Run With the Wolves.

To be welcomed into the camp of the wild warrior women, the

priestesses who have made the decision not to become bitter in the face of life's broken promises, is an invitation into the cauldron of wisdom that lives in the body of women.

To be shown the power of the purity of the feminine heart. Purity that comes from the undoing of life's seeming wrongs, to a heart educated through grief, rather than bowed by it, holding that grief, knowing in time it will turn to praise. Revealing the purity that lies beneath from the beginning, not something recreated, something that has just got covered in the dust and clutter of life, that is always there. To be held by the fierce and gentle power of feminine inclusivity. Women sharing a heart full of gratitude, for the fullness of life, for the paradox that it appears to be.

Then if this does not happen if there is no inclusive circle of empowered women to support the growth through life, or there is no self-actualising, because the pain and trauma has overwhelmed that person and the story seems more real than reality.

"When a woman is frozen of feeling, when she can no longer feel herself, when her blood, her passion, no longer reach the extremities of her psyche, when she is desperate; then a fantasy life is far more pleasurable than anything else she can set her sights upon. Her little match lights, because they have no wood to burn, instead burn up the psyche as though it were a big dry log. The psyche begins to play tricks on itself; it lives now in the fantasy fire of all yearning fulfilled. This kind of fantasizing is like a lie: If you tell it often enough, you begin to believe it."
Clarissa Pinkola Estés, Women Who Run With the Wolves.

When the old patterns of rites of passage are undergone and as youths there is an introduction to the inner landscapes we experience and a feeling of coming home to the Earth, then we can live with vitality and connection. Growing in love for our surroundings, our earth and each other. Through this, wisdom grows with age and when we are struggling there are elders there to support us.

I remember visiting my aunt Ursula, after the breakdown of the relationship with the mother of my first child. In my mind the fairy tale had been broken. Ursula, who must have been in her eighties then, was the least judgmental, of all those I shared with at that time.

If there is a deep connection to nature and spirit, then spirit guides and nature can be turned to for support and guidance as well as the elders. This process of becoming wise means that the elders once they pass across to the other side, may have the capacity to assist from there.

"We do not die alone

We die to the state our heart has grown."

CONVERSATIONS WITH THE ANCESTORS

I recently ran a workshop called conversations with the ancestors; I felt it was necessary to share some of the experiences that have unfolded for me with my own ancestors, that have shown me what their role is with the living. I wanted to try to help people understand the nature of their relationship with their birth ancestors, with the ancestors of place and the grand ancestors, or spirit powers of the directions.

I began with a question; "How many of you have had an experience of your dead parent or grandparent?". Ninety five percent of the thirty or so participants put up their hands. "Workshop over" I declared, "You can go home". What this showed me is that they were already having this conversation, but like the greater conversation with nature, it is not really accepted within society as a part of natural life. It is considered super-natural.

"In the culture of my people, the Dagara, we have no word for the supernatural. The closest we come to this concept is Yielbongura, 'the thing that knowledge can't eat.'
This word suggests that the life and power of certain things depend upon their resistance to the kind of categorizing knowledge that human beings apply to everything.
In Western reality, there is a clear split between the spiritual and the material, between religious life and secular life. This concept is alien to

the Dagara. For us, as for many indigenous cultures, the supernatural is part of our everyday lives.
To a Dagara man or woman, the material is just the spiritual taking on form. The secular is religion in a lower key — a rest area from the tension of religious and spiritual practice."
Malidoma Patrice Somé

As Malidoma says, there is no separation between spirit and the 'normal' world, all aspects are present, we are just culturally steered away from this notion. Then our spiritual life can be kept out of our own hands i.e. in the hands of priests, monks and teachers and away from the broad expanse of our lives. So it is only a rarefied separate experience for a few hours a week, or a single peak experience.

I did continue with the conversation with the ancestors and the next question took us deeper. "How many of you can unequivocally tell me which ancestor it was that showed up", I continued. This time only five people put up their hands. Four of them told of how supportive their ancestors were, how they turned up in times of turmoil or gently offered their heartfelt support. The fifth told of how when her mother's spirit showed up, the television would come on at 2 am, how she would lose her keys, and how a litany of things would go wrong. It was clear her mother's spirit was still in a lot of pain, and needed some healing. I suggested this to the woman who had shared her experience. She, with a great deal of honesty said: " I don't want to heal her, I have the power now!". She explained how awful her mother had been to her.

This whole interaction was extremely useful, as it showed how the spirit world is; part benign and part malignant; with the malignant part of spirit consisting of spirits that are acting from a place of pain, whether they are ancestral spirits or other spirits. This helps to show that relating to the unseen can be through, learning and healing or fearfully ignoring.

We also got a picture of the main function of the ancestral spirits, that they are there to help and support us or need healing. This has always been my experience and helped me to understand how ancient people related to the ancestors. It was not that they worshiped them, but that they were still taking care of them, because they felt they had not gone very far. This starts to show why ancestral lands are of such importance to earth based people. And huge anguish has been caused by moving tribes from the lands they have always lived on. It is an immense religious/spiritual sacrilege, and has caused a great deal of harm to all earth based people who have suffered this. From Australian Aboriginals, who were classed as flora and fauna until 1964 and who were relocated and subjected to the western dehumanising education. Also America's first people have suffered immensely from these issues, with this lack of understanding even happening to this day with the Dakota pipe line. This has gone on under the guise of progress, in Africa and Asia for generations, and these type of cultural traumas, create a culture of trauma, which is what we are currently living in. Those who are traumatized, learn and practice the same ways to perpetuate trauma on others, unless the cycle is broken.

Coming out of this cycle, means shedding generations of story and victimhood in order to become empowered. Yet how many of us are defined by our trauma, and would feel naked and scared if we were not clothed in our trauma, our story? There have been some amazing examples of people who have managed this; Nelson Mandela, Emmeline Pankhurst, John Trudel, Kathleen Cleaver, Dr Martin Luther King, Gandhi, Ai Weiwei, Russell Means and many more.

The respect that is required for the bones of our ancestors, is no longer something we consider in our disconnected age. Even in the U.K. we have a strange anomaly, of the bones of our ancient ancestors put on display at Stonehenge. Unless we can show our genealogical connection to them, it is unlikely they will be given the respect they deserve. This type of sacrilege is no longer tolerated by America's first people, Maori and native Hawaiian's.

There are ways in which we can show our respect and acknowledgement of our ancestors. When I lived as a student in a shared house. One of the inhabitants was a Nigerian and whenever food fell on the floor, he would say that the ancestors were hungry. I thought this was beautiful and adopted this at that time. There are more formal ways of doing this, like making an ancestor plate of food and leaving it out for them. This Ancestor worship or Ancestor reverence as I prefer to call it, exists in many traditions and among most peoples. From Celtic, (Samhain), Christian, (All saints day and All hallows, or Halloween) Mayan, Aborigine, Native American, African, Hindu, Chinese and In Mexico with the celebration of the day of the dead.

"I have found many moments of joy and contentment when I am in communion with my father and my ancestors. They laugh with me, they send me messages in the wind, they sail in on the wings of a hawk, they comfort me with love and provide loving guidance for my soul's path in this life. This requires personal work - to dissolve old programming, emotions, grudges and stories - and it continues to require these shifts. For me, ancestral communication and healing has been the most powerful and rewarding gift of my spiritual journey."

Michael Shankara

One of the issues raised here is that we need to have sorted out our emotional business with our ancestors, to open a road for clear communication. Just before my father died, I trained with him in Polarity therapy, spending more time with him over the six month training, than over the previous six years. During this time I had one conversation with him where we met as men ,not as father and son, in which we sorted out our emotional business, especially what had built up over the previous four years. This meant that when he passed very suddenly, I was only left feeling grief and eventually love, as there was no unfinished business.

My father died when he was fifty four, he drowned in Australia saving a German woman, who had got into trouble in a rip tide. He was a strong swimmer and his power animal was Dolphin. He had swum with dolphins on that same beach the year before. In the year after he died I had a number of dreams in which he appeared, until in the last one, I confided in him that we would have to return the life insurance. After tha,t he did not return in my dreams and his spirit only returned several years later. A year after he died I was on the cliffs over Senen Cove in Cornwall and ten dolphins swam past, the only time I had ever seen this many dolphins in the U.K.

When my father's spirit returned, he told me that he had returned to help the family. I sent him to support various members of the family and each time I got swift and positive responses from them about his help. When he turned up and everyone seemed fine, I decided to send him to help his best friend who was going through a divorce. It felt like, he, his wife and their children were all part of our family. I sent my father's spirit off to Carlisle where his best friend lived. After a few days I got curious, and called. His wife answered, "Is Dan there?" I asked, "No, he is in Cuba", she replied. Oops I thought, I screwed up there and forgot about it. Several months later ,I was talking to Dan on the phone and he told me many of his Cuban adventures. Just as we were about to end the call I asked, "Did you meet my father's spirit when you were in Cuba?". There was a long pause and then Dan told me a story he was not planning to tell me. "I met a Yoruban shaman while I was there, who invited me to a ceremony. During the ceremony he came to me and said that 'Mare' (Maria) 'The spirit of the sea', had come with a friend. This friend had told him that, 'He was thinking of Dan when he died.'. This left me with a deep sense of gratitude; What a beautiful thing to say to your best friend from the other side.

There are a number of experiences of this kind that I have had that have showed me how our ancestors can be supporting us. This has formed my understanding of ancestor reverence and the need for this part of the conversation in spirit to be engaged with.

TRUE NATURE

As children we play out doors in nature or are lucky enough to be mentored in connecting with nature, we discover or are shown what to pay attention to. The tracks, the voices of the birds, the so called weeds, we can eat and use for medicines and so much more. We make fires and dens and feel at home on the Earth.

This can develop into an understanding of being in the flow of nature through stalking. Through this practice, experiences are available that can allow the mirror like aspect of the natural world to become apparent, as slowing down means the birds and animals start to show themselves, reflecting our capacity to move in the flow. This practice also produces an inner stillness that is available, stopping the incessant parade of thought through the mind. The doorway to a level of oneness is available. Through entering the flow state, greater connection can be reached, it can even become the preferred state, accessible in natural and urban settings alike. This natural brainwave state, becoming a choice that brings greater adsorption, silencing the mind, reducing anxiety and inner conflict, putting a stop to unsolicited thought, 'stopping the world'.

Following the practice of tracking curiosity and awareness grow. The capacity to ask skillful questions of life is then an everyday enquiry. Firstly this awareness is directed to the outward mysteries and this subtly shifts to all the inner mysteries as well. This facilitates the great conversation with the natural world and enriches each day, bringing awe and gratitude.

When imagination directs the body's energy, there is the possibility that the principle that 'Mind moves energy' becomes experientially understood. With this, a connection is forged with the energy that moves in and through all things, and a quality of playful experimentation deepens the natural conversation. As long as no harm is done towards another, we are free to play here.

Awareness is the doorway to spirit, so these findings beyond the physical can naturally lead to a deeper inquiry, where connection with spirit of place, guides and ancestors unfolds. Perhaps guidance is sought, in how to access these realms with safety and for the benefit of others. This can feel like a natural unfolding, a discovery of the full spectrum of being human.

TRUE NATURE

When spiritual development starts with a requirement for belief instead of belief resting on experience, the cart is being put before the horse. It is a kind of blindness that allows those who represent spiritual and religious organisations a have a get out of jail free card.

Belief in ideas that are not our experience, set up an internal cognitive dissonance, whatever the belief is it is unlikely to be what is being experienced. This means it encourages a split between thought and experience, which moves us further away from an experience of oneness. Belief based on experience however becomes unshakable, because the belief has become knowledge.

When the mind acts like an internal puppet show, with different characters trying to be heard and continuously trying to be helpful in a very unhelpful way. The myriad voices in the mind can be reduced down to two main categories. The first: unhelpfully reminds us we are a piece of shit at all times, undermining every triumph, expressed in the voice of the critic, the parent, the cynic, the know it all, the teacher, etc…playing on self-doubt, depression and lack of self-love, creating thoughts that are so abhorrent, that just because they passed through the mind it feels like it has somehow tainted the purity of the soul. The second is uplifting, claiming angelic status, for the self ,not being really of this place, above it all and special, justifying the point of view that is held, continuously putting the self in the right. This creates continuous internal conflict, while an external defense of personal territory is taking place as well. We find that self-diminishment or self-aggrandisement amount to the same thing, the strengthening of the story of self, the strengthening of the ego.

Yet there is a place for the ego, it is needed to develop the story of self, in order to be active in the world, though there comes a time when letting go of it is crucial to our return to the unconditioned self. When the self is traumatised a compassionate act might be to help rearrange the deck chairs on the proverbial deck of the Titanic, to create more internal space. Yet the ego at some point may merge into the vastness of the ocean.

When we believe either of the opposing voices, we are caught by the net of the mind in the duality of the imaginary self. Not realising that the internal dialogue is really a monologue. The mind is a master of creating self-conflict and the longer it keeps this up the longer the construct of the self continues. The longer the physical mind is in charge. If the thoughts are not believed then they eventually stop, with no audience to witness the inner drama silence prevails. This incessant disruption of thought is like ripples on the surface of the water, blocking our capacity to look more deeply into the river, in to what is actually happening.

There is a practice from the Irish Bardic tradition where a member of the clan was selected. One year from the selection, they would be sat in a chair and have reflected back to them any of the things they had done that year, their behaviour and even wild rumors. This took place in front of the whole clan. On the first night of this, they could not respond and if they managed to stay in the chair throughout the day they got a reward of some kind. The following night they could respond. This practice is a skillful way of inviting the person to pay precise attention to their behavior, in order to be able to ascertain for themselves the truth or otherwise of their actions, in the face of intense scrutiny. This leads to impeccability and becoming ultimately responsible for one's own energy.

When in relationship with another there is a close reflection of each other, this observation might turn to criticism or accusation. This presents a perfect place to be practicing a level of inner awareness, that tries to witness all the inner processes that are taking place. In the same way that stalking slows down the body, meditation has the capacity to slow down the mind, so we can see accurately what is happening.

We may notice how we have a thought about the other, this triggers a feeling and a story starts to develop that we are telling ourselves; in effect we are making the whole thing up. It may be that we have an uncomfortable feeling, that we attribute to the behaviour of the other and again the story starts to roll, like a snowball until it is out of our control and takes over avalanching in a display of emotion we are buried in. We may have intuitive feelings that are accurate, that give us information, if so we need to be able to distinguish this from our fantasy, by some skillful means.

This inner attention, starts to help us to recognize, first, in the self ,how conflict and drama arise and then in others. When explaining this to another, it can provoke the response that their feelings are not being validated. It is worth remembering that our feelings are real, but they are not reality. When a feeling is triggered, it is happening in us and emerges from our collected lifelong patterns. It belongs to us, we ultimately get to choose how we respond, to whatever the stimulus is. Though this depends on how much space there is within i.e. how slowed down the inner processes are, to be able to have time to choose a response.

We are responsible only for this arising in the self and may or may not be able to communicate this to others. As the dust settles with in the emptiness of mind that can emerge from this recognition, there is a universal and deep level of compassion, it is just there, because when the self-conflicted mind and the suffering it creates through self-storytelling are witnessed, it is possible to see how this affliction creates all suffering and affects almost everyone. There is a recognition that in creating these thought stories about the other and the world, we are not experiencing things clearly. Our mind and body are not synchronised, the involvement with the thought drama, triggers powerful emotions that create tides of chemicals in the body, that we become addicted to. There is a habituation towards certain emotional responses and the associated chemistry that they trigger. In order to feel normal there is a recreation of these familiar patterns. Patterns that might relate to family situations from the distant past.

With the warrior's understanding of good and bad; as in the story of the Taoist farmer, that we cannot possibly know which is which. As what was the best thing that happened to us in the past, can become the worst. And while in the process of it going bad, valuable lessons could be learned. Which is it then, good or bad? The warrior adopts the view that it is all interesting and then curiosity undoes the dualistic judgement of events. The effect of this is to dissipate drama around and within the warrior. This is not about morals, it is about undoing the subliminal and conscious judgements that empower the stories we tell ourselves.

This leads to an eerie emptiness, the feeling of which can be like something between, boredom and depression. It feels like an emotional cul de sac. Emptiness is not a feeling that is sought, it is often profoundly terrifying,, as there is a propensity to fill any space with something or other. With the habituation towards all the chemistry emotions release in the body and the many masks and roles that have been adopted, this feeling of nakedness is alarming, as there is nowhere to hide from the experience of self.

Then as nothing continues to happen, it becomes almost dull that nothing is happening, there are no feelings in the space. We are used to feeling things all the time, mostly in a reactive way, 'you make me feel like this', we say. It is different in the space, feeling has an emergent quality it is not linked to actions. There is recognition that what has been felt is a contrast of emotion. Somewhat like the self-conflict of the mind, our heart has been a place of one feeling contrasted against another.

At some point beyond the story, the compassionate heart wakes and a joyful heart centered quality unfolds, that seems to underpin all feeling. With an empty mind, heart fullness becomes the preferred choice. So called negative emotions, impinge from time to time causing a constriction in the heart field, though they feel quite constricting and painful and as such are easily recognised and moved through.

In most spiritual traditions, the sentiment is expressed that everything you need is inside. This is true. There is also a saying in Zen 'inside and outside the same' this is also true. If meditation techniques are practiced that only focus our attention internally, there is less focus on the development of external awareness. Getting off the meditation cushion and returning to the external world ,the state of meditation will be tested by what happens. What can be found when working with both inner and outer techniques, is that sending attention in or expanding it out brings it ultimately to the same place. There is the capacity to meet in our inner worlds, as much as there is a capacity to meet in the outer world. There are exercises that can be run that allow shared inner experiences to be corroborated by both parties. And as remote viewing illustrates, it is possible to view the real world by sending our spiritual self out, even meeting in spirit form at certain pre designated spots on the physical landscape.

These pursuits are all going on within the emptiness. When bird language is taught, it is asked of us that we listen to the silence, as then all the bird song can be heard. Similarly if attention is put on to the emptiness, then all the phenomena acting within the emptiness can be experienced. Normally the people and things in the space take our attention far too readily to notice what is already there and what unifies and underpins everything.

One of the main stories that we tell ourselves is that, 'We are not loved enough'. There is a tendency to, therefore, try to find that love outside of the self. This search for love outside the self comes with the possibility of blaming others for not making us happy, when our happiness is our own responsibility. The reminder of the notion that all we need is inside is a clue to how this is expressed and how we can feel what is happening.

We have a body this is the Earth loving us into being. The phosphorous, (amongst other elements), that make up our bones, was made in the stars; this is the whole universe conspiring to love us into being. Oh, and we are a spirit in a physical body, this is the Spirit world telling us it loves us….

When the experience of being loved into being flows through us daily, we come to relationships very differently. There is no longer a grasping for love from the other ,there is a bringing of love and seeking to engender a similar self-loving experience in the other. So a celebration of the journey can be fully made.

This universe loves you

In the vastness of space

A heart beats to the rhythm of love

Birthed by a harmonious spirit song

The flesh that surrounds it

Is the love of the Earth

The bones that animate it

Is the love of the stars

The blood that flows through it

Is a river of love

Its very existence is the proof of love

And all this is happening in you too

And you ask me if I love you

And I say the whole universe loves you

And you say, you are being evasive

Ok I say this universe loves you.

(To Ariel Blue)

BECOMING

If you want to know something then become it. This understanding is a path way into nature and survival. To find water we become water, to hunt the deer we become it, to understand another being we become them. I have related several of these experiences and the overriding effect of this process is twofold. we begin to understand that we can put our mind/spirit into anything and through this we loosen the over identification with self, by discovering our consciousness is much bigger than can fit in a human body. There is an expansion into the experience of being a lot more than a human. In John Perkins book shapeshifting, he explains that the main reason people struggle to shape shift is because they are too worried that they won't come back to being a human. This is largely because they do not recognise that all the entities of the Earth are conscious in their own way. Perhaps not conscious in the same way as humans, but infused with their own concerns and purposes. We have become very human centric in our thinking and have moved away from a relationship with the wider family. It is time to be reembraced by our family and for us to recognise and enjoy the sentience of the flow of life that supports us, that we are a part of not apart from.

"While much psychology emphasizes the familial causes of angst in humans, the cultural component carries as much weight, for culture is the family of the family. If the family of the family has various sicknesses, then all families within that culture will have to struggle with the same malaises. There is a saying cultura cura, culture cures. If the culture is a healer, the families learn how to heal; they will struggle less, be more reparative, far less wounding, far more graceful and loving. In a culture where the predator rules, all new life needing to be born, all old life needing to be gone, is unable to move and the soul-lives of its citizenry are frozen with both fear and spiritual famine." Clarissa Pinkola Estés, Women Who Run With the Wolves.

Separation from nature and the great conversation is eating our soul and sanctioning the destruction of our living home. We need to move out of the place of being lost, by not knowing our Earth and how to live on it, to become a caretaker. There is a need to wake up to the full spectrum human that we are; existing as a physical, energetic and spiritual being. We may even heed the quiet voice of spirit, the ancestors and nature. We can celebrate the journey with our earthly and celestial relations. We can take the road of transforming our trauma, making grief a skill and moving from grief to praise. We can integrate our innocent and magical child self with the fully fledged broken hearted warrior, to make a soft and powerful, curious and tenderly present, human being. A warrior of the heart. We can stop believing the dual nature of mind and find the reflective peace that brings us into spaciousness. Through the practice of stalking, we can stop the world and master the self.

There is a pressing need for us all to do what we can, there are seven billion caretakers on this planet and if we all chipped in we could sort all the problems out in a short time.

We are an expression of natural phenomena, that flow through the fabric of consciousness. States that we may call: physical, energetic, spiritual or void. This expression is not a fixed self, it is beyond time, it is beyond imagining. This is also not referring to some far of destination, it is very close, so close we are breathing it daily. Like a fish that does not notice the water in which it swims. To separate ourselves from the flow of consciousness or from nature is impossible. This is a call to connect with the natural self, to remember the wild self, the part that is merged with the natural world, that becomes one with it, that is inseparable from it, our true nature.

"What he said, not only explained the world of inner vision but also touched on the 'oneness' he often spoke of. He said "If a rabbit moved on your back, could you not feel it? There is no separation in the force of nature, no inner or outer dimension; we are at once part of nature and nature is part of us." It took me many years to understand that profound statement and many more years to do what he had done."

Tom Brown Jr The vision p58

TRUE NATURE

Printed in Great Britain
by Amazon

24554246R00136